RATHLIN - N

Ecologist and writer Philip V
fifty years, spending lengthy
fisheries, engaging in wildlife ɛ
folklore. In this lively and pers...... ....., ...
writing, memoir and a trawl of tales to share his enthusiasm for this
unique island. This book completes the author's trilogy featuring
The Giant's Causeway, the Antrim Coast and Rathlin Island.

RATHLIN

NATURE & FOLKLORE

PHILIP WATSON

STONE COUNTRY

This edition published by
Stone Country Press Ltd
61 Sinclair Drive
Glasgow
G42 9PU

www.stonecountry.co.uk

ISBN 978-0-9548779-8-9

A catalogue record for this book is available
from the British Library

Map by Philip Watson
Design by Stone Country

CONTENTS

MAP... vi

PREFACE... 8

INTRODUCTION... 11

PART ONE: NATURE

1. TO THE LIGHTHOUSE...14

2. DROPPING A LINE...25

3. WHERE THE STONES SPEAK...44

4. GREEN IS MY VALLEY...57

5. ISLAND FLOWER GARDEN...65

6. WETLANDS...89

7. BUTTERFLIES AND MOTHS...94

8. FUR AND FEATHERS...100

9. THE WATER MARGIN...114

10. THE SURROUNDING SEA...125

11. UNDER THE WAVES...128

12. WHIRRING MULTITUDES...137

13. SELCHIES AND LEVIATHANS...150

PART TWO: FOLKLORE

14. FOLKLORE ON RATHLIN...155

15. PLACE NAMES...157

16. FOLKLORE AND NATURE...162

17. SUPERSTITIONS & BELIEF...202

PART THREE: THEN AND NOW

18. STRANGE BEHAVIOURS...210

19. ALL CHANGE...220

REFERENCES...228

ACKNOWLEDGEMENTS...234

APPENDICES...237

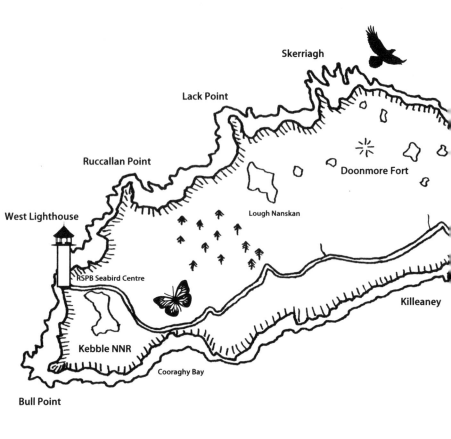

Skerriagh

Lack Point

Ruccallan Point

Doonmore Fort

West Lighthouse

Lough Nanskan

RSPB Seabird Centre

Killeaney

Kebble NNR

Cooraghy Bay

Bull Point

0	1 Km	1 Mile

RATHLIN

This sketch map is for general information and routes shown are approximate. For more detailed information, refer to Ordnance Survey Northern Ireland Discoverer Map Series 1:50,000 Sheet 5 (Ballycastle)

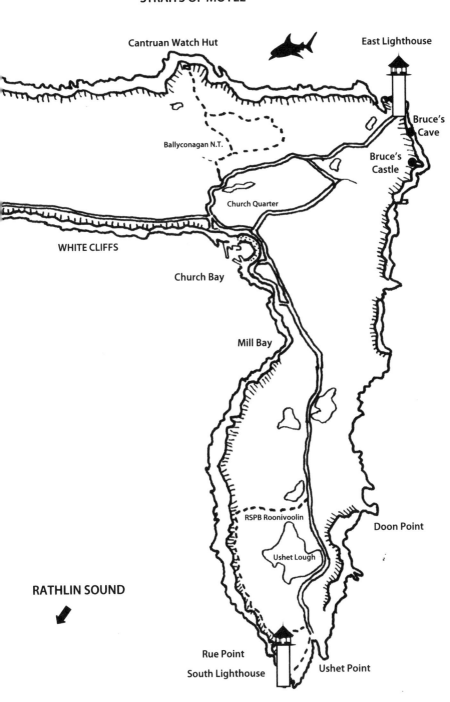

STRAITS OF MOYLE

Cantruan Watch Hut

East Lighthouse

Bruce's Cave

Bruce's Castle

Ballyconagan N.T.

Church Quarter

WHITE CLIFFS

Church Bay

Mill Bay

RSPB Roonivoolin

Doon Point

Ushet Lough

RATHLIN SOUND

Rue Point

South Lighthouse

Ushet Point

PREFACE

Being On An Island

What do we expect when visiting an island? An experience of somewhere different from the mainland; a feeling of isolation; peace and quiet; the frisson of worry mixed with the anticipation of a Robinson Crusoe adventure such that, if the weather changes for the worse, we might be marooned.

Ireland is an island, but if you live in Athlone for example – slap-bang in the centre – you don't pick up any island feeling. You need to be on a smallish island to get the right perception. On Rathlin, all your senses are stimulated by the sea; you can see it all around you from any high point, smell the marine tang, taste the salt on the wind, feel the shudder as waves crash on to the shore and explode against the cliffs, hear the roar of tide rips and cries of seabirds and seals. You are left in no doubt that you are on an island, and that for me is a great feeling and one which I hope this book will share with you.

This is not a guidebook, although readers will find information on where to see wildlife and discover folklore surviving in an oral tradition, some of which has been collected and published in specific journals perhaps not known to many. If the book is to be classified, then it is about an island; its landscape, nature, folklore and a significant element of personal memoir. It reflects my interests and therefore some sections are longer than others, thus any bias towards particular topics and equally any omissions and errors, are my responsibility.

I begin with what tempted me to Rathlin - bird migration then fisheries work. These are followed by geology, because this influences most of what follows, for example: agriculture, flora, freshwater and the fauna. Then it is gradually down to the sea via the seashore and the shallows, the sea itself, the seabirds, seals and whales and what lives permanently underwater. There follows the folklore section, which looks at storytelling on the island, then in more detail at folklore in relation to nature, finishing with an examination of superstitions and beliefs. Finally, there is a short history of naturalists on Rathlin over the past 200 years or so and then a concluding essay on the rise of tourism and conservation.

The debt I owe to Rathlin islanders and others in putting together this book is large. I have pestered many friends and acquaintances both on the island and off it for information gathered over many generations, all of whom are acknowledged. There is a fine division between research and intrusion. The poet Seamus Heaney quotes (2010) a Roman text which advises that we should be careful when transferring what we know to writing and this is something I have been aware of throughout my times on Rathlin and while writing this book. The following quotes and references are apt:

> *"Well the natives didn't really take to me, perhaps because I argued so, so in the end I gave up conversation and took to writing in my notebook and they liked that less, especially when I did it on a Sunday. And they think it just impertinent when one goes around asking for statistics."*

> *"Hetty to Maisie", in 'I Crossed The Minch', Louis MacNeice, (1938)*

During his visits to the Hebrides described in the above, MacNeice, looking for a hermit's residence, was quizzed by a Berneray angler:

"Fishing?"
"No, not fishing."
"Not trying to get information, are you?"
"No," I said quickly.

Tim Robinson, describing his fieldwork on the Aran Islands off western Ireland, which led to the two volumes of *Stones of Aran* (1989, 1997), admitted that a degree of patience and cunning was required in persuading island farmers and fishermen to unlock their memories.

Finally, this comment from one of a crew of three North Antrim fishermen at the end of my first season's work with them investigating lobsters and crabs. I had expressed my frustration with the ambiguous answers they provided to my questions about their fishing practices and catches: *"Well, you see, you could have been the taxman for all we knew."*

Over the subsequent years suspicions evaporated, trust was won and friendship established. Such privileges must be earned – you can't rush these things.

INTRODUCTION

Island of Ghosts and Guillemots

Rathlin today is vibrant, busy, receiving thousands of summer visitors – be they humans or seabirds – gets on with life and looks to the future with confidence. It was not always so – if anywhere can lay claim to harbouring ghosts, then the 'disputed island', as it was known, can offer a history of massacres and other tragic events as turbulent as the tides that swirl and boil around its shores.

Shipwrecks, drownings, slaying of islanders by Vikings, Scottish clans and English forces (including Francis Drake), famine, emigration – the list of momentous times in Rathlin's recorded human history is long and varied. It is not within the scope of this book to examine these, and readers seeking pointers to Rathlin's history will find some in the references. There are several published accounts of the island's ancient and more recent histories, including four by islanders, and historical and archaeological studies are adding to information on Rathlin's past. Perhaps the definitive history of the island is still to be written. If ghosts exist then Rathlin with its turbulent past must be a rich haunting ground. So far ghost hunters, including professionals, have had some lively times on the island but have yet to deliver any evidence.

A few basic statistics will give readers an introduction. Rathlin Island is situated off the North Coast of County Antrim in Northern Ireland. Its nearest Scottish neighbours are the Mull of Kintyre and the islands of Islay and Jura. Rathlin is Northern Ireland's only permanently inhabited offshore island, occupied for at least 7000 years. Some islanders still refer to it as *Raghery;* an old name also known on the main Antrim coast. Early writers such as Pliny (77 AD) described an island between Ireland and Britain, known as Riginia, and Ptolemy (about 150 AD) mentioned Rhikinia. In the seventh century it was referred to as *Rechru.* Clark (1996) has a useful appendix on all this by Dr A.B. Taylor. The name *Rathlin*, in modern use, has also existed for centuries.

The island's distance offshore from County Antrim, and its length, seems to vary according to which book or article you read. It is a relatively simple task, with a pair of dividers and the 1:50,000 (one inch) Ordnance Survey map of the Ballycastle area, to get the measure of Rathlin. The island's three lighthouses are useful reference points. The ferry route, under normal conditions, from Ballycastle to Church Bay harbour is 10 kilometres (6 miles). The nearest point at Fair Head on the mainland to Rue Point at the southern tip of Rathlin is 4 kms (2.5 miles). Similarly, from Kenbane Head just west of Ballycastle to Bull Point at the island's western tip is 7 kms (4.25 miles).

The island lies about 21 kms (13 miles) from the Mull of Kintyre in Scotland. Rathlin's highest point is 136 metres (447 feet) above sea level; the island is L-shaped – from East Light to Rue Point Light on the south arm is 5 kms (3 miles) and from East Light to the West Light on the west arm is just over 7 kms (4.5 miles). The narrowest part is 0.8 kms (0.5 miles) wide and the broadest 2 kms (1.25 miles). Distances by roads are a little longer and information on signposts varies according to where they are situated. As you walk or cycle the island you realise that its contours add much to your effort. The total area, including lakes, is about 1420 hectares (3500 acres).

The title of this brief introduction is a reminder that the book is about Rathlin's natural and un-natural histories, including natural resources and their uses, and folklore relating to these, although good stories – about ghosts or otherwise - are not ignored. The guillemot is a brown and white seabird, the most numerous bird on Rathlin during the months from May through to the end of August. A detailed census of seabirds on Rathlin in 1999 produced a total of just under 96,000 guillemots inhabiting the cliffs and rock stacks in May and June of that year, along with tens of thousands of other seabirds. Recent declines in some of these species have not lessened the amazing spectacle of what Victorian visitors to the island called 'whirring multitudes'. The seabirds also have their place in the island's folklore, as will be revealed later.

It is difficult to believe that fifty years have passed since my first footsteps on Rathlin, for those first days remain memorable and I have no need to refer to notes or journals to begin with the journey to the lighthouse.

PART ONE - NATURE

1. TO THE LIGHTHOUSE

Crossing the Sound

I first saw Rathlin Island fifty years ago in May 1960 from the 200 metre (a little over 600 ft) high cliff top of Fair Head, at Ireland's north-east corner. A twitchy teenage birdwatcher, I was on the headland to spot Ireland's only pair of breeding golden eagles. The island shone in the sun then quite quickly fragmented and vanished under a sea mist. I sensed its allure and wished to go there. Three months later, a friend invited me to join an expedition to Rathlin to set up a bird observatory and my wish came true.

Following that first view of Rathlin, it is August and I am looking at her again, this time from the small pier at Ballycastle, waiting while the ferryman chides us about the amount of luggage our party has dumped beside the mail boat he runs between this north Antrim resort and the island.

Half an hour out from Ballycastle harbour the little boat pitches and tosses in the *slough-na-mara* ('hollow of the sea'), a notorious tide rip in Rathlin Sound. The boat is low in the water, weighed down by our party of eight, our rucsacs, supplies for two months and sections of wooden bunk-beds for the sparsely furnished lighthouse cottage that is our destination. White cliffs of chalk gleam and towers of black basalt glower, then all vanish as we plough into a trough of green water.

Thankfully we rise again and the island's long arms reach out in an angular embrace and we reach the safety of the small harbour in Church Bay.

We've come north to Rathlin – you can't get any further north in Northern Ireland – but others are heading south on a course that will bring them to meet us: the late summer and autumn migrations of birds from Greenland, Iceland and Scandanavia is just beginning. Birds from the north-west will come to Rathlin over the sea, perhaps island-hopping down by way of the Faroes, Iceland and the Hebrides, although many may make their landfall at Inishowen and north-west Donegal; those from the north-east may follow the long arm of the Kintyre peninsula that points to Ireland; some from further east can be drifted off-course by unfavourable winds and come to Rathlin, while others, after perhaps making landfalls at Fair Isle and the Shetlands, may re-align themselves south and come down the west coast of Scotland towards the island. We are a party of mainly young birdwatchers and enthusiasts for bird migration, hoping to find out more about these birds of passage, but first we need a roof over our sea-wet heads.

Birds on the Move

Rathlin's East Light is one of three lighthouses on the island. The first to be built, it perches on the edge of Altacarry Head on the north-east corner of the island, the light itself 74 metres (240 ft) above the sea. It began operations in 1856 and today it shows four flashes of white light every 20 seconds, operating over 24 hours. We have permission from the Commissioners of Irish Lights in Dublin (who oversee all lights around the entire coast of Ireland) to stay at one of the small lighthouse cottages (only one cottage remains now) within the compound where the lighthouse keepers live.

It takes us the rest of the daylight hours to assemble the bunk beds and prepare a meal, and after our journey and this work, we are glad to turn in and sleep. Sometime in the early hours of the next morning, a terrific bang wakes us. Before anyone is truly sensible, another thunderous explosion shakes the cottage. We run about in the dark, bumping into each other and asking what is going on. BOOM! This time we make it to the front door, just in time to recoil from a further explosion. It is the lighthouse fog gun, used to warn passing ships; a charge of explosive is swung out over the sea wall on a gantry and detonated – twice every five minutes - sending a crack echoing across the waves and reverberating around the walled compound of the lighthouse and the dwellings. A sharp smell of cordite hangs in the misty air. The lighthouse keeper on duty explains the procedure, amused at our initial panic. Today the fog warning is a radio signal.

Our attention is quickly diverted from the fog gun to the lighthouse. In the low cloud, rain and mist, the great beams of white light cut the air like swords, and in the light we see the silvery flashes of wings. Hundreds of night-flying migrant birds are swirling around the light, confused and dazzled. Many scrabble against the thick glass of the lantern room and some crash into it and fall stunned on the narrow platform that encircles the light. We rush up the tower staircase and find starlings, thrushes, wheatears, robins, tiny warblers and others flying through the spears of light. With the stars obscured by thick cloud and fog, these travellers have lost a key navigational cue and come to the brightest light they can see – the slowly circling beams of the lighthouse. I feel the flutter of heartbeats as we put exhausted birds in cotton bags and take them back to the cottage to recover.

Next day, we take notes on plumage, moult, weights and measurements, then put a numbered light aluminium ring on a leg of the birds and release them. Other migrants are caught about the island on subsequent days in fine-meshed nets and are also ringed. In this way, the migration paths and destinations of birds can be discovered, as some of these ringed birds are recovered and information flows in to a central body coordinating such work.

Two small wading birds ringed in 1960 and 1961 were recovered subsequently in Spain and France respectively, so indeed Rathlin is a stopping point, voluntary or enforced by bad weather, for birds on their autumn (and spring) migrations. We hear nothing of the fate of the warblers and other little land birds, bound for the Mediterranean and Africa, following their own mental maps and guided by stars more reliable than Rathlin's small constellation of lighthouses.

Bad weather and the disorientating effect of lighthouses are only two of the many hazards birds face during migrations. Songbirds suffer huge annual losses; hundreds of millions of individuals are trapped or shot – particularly in the Mediterranean flyways – during the spring and autumn movements between Africa and Eurasia. Much of this hunting is illegal and contrary to European Union environmental laws. Some European countries have strong traditions of taking songbirds for food or shooting them for so-called sport. As enforcement of the laws against these activities is variable at best, conservation organisations are tackling this problem by a programme of education and raising awareness in the hope that cultural isolation will bring such slaughter to an end.

Case Study - The Wheatear

The wheatear is a small grey and brown bird between a robin and a thrush in size. It has a vivid white base to its tail, near the rump. Its name is derived from the Old English *hwit aers* meaning 'white arse'. What's really remarkable about this bouncy chat with a liking for rocky places (it's in the group of birds known as chats, small members of the thrush tribe, that includes our well known stonechat) is its migration. Weighing about 30 grams (an ounce) this little bag of feathers, fat, blood and bones, with a brain the size of a thumbnail, finds its way from summer sites in Siberia to winter grounds in Central Africa, a round trip of 25-30,000 km (15,625 – 18,750 miles). Wheatears summering in North-Eastern Canada and the ice-free areas of Greenland cross 1,500 to 2,000 km (937 – 1,250 miles) of Atlantic Ocean to get to Europe and on to Africa's warmth for winter. Some have invaded Alaska from Siberia by crossing the Bering Strait. Even these summer Yanks go to Africa in winter.

You could say that places like Siberia, Alaska, Greenland and Northern Canada would drive anyone to the heat of Africa, but the truth is – it was from that continent that wheatears, and humans, spread north and colonised the northern hemisphere, following the retreating ice during the warmer interglacial periods as new territories opened up for prospectors.

I'd known that some birds migrated, but it was catching the slightly larger and more strongly coloured Greenland variety of the wheatear at the East Lighthouse on wet, foggy nights in August 1960 that brought home to me the incredible journeys these little birds make. I felt the tremble of life and looked into that dark eye that peered back at me, dazzled in the beams of the light. Here was a bird, small in my hand, which had just flown across the North Atlantic, or no less incredibly, island-hopped via Iceland and the Faroes to Ireland, onward bound to cross the Sahara Desert and settle somewhere south to catch flies around an African villager herding his cattle through dusty scrub.

How does it find its way? Why doesn't it fly south down the east coast of the USA and winter in the New World tropics? That would half its present odyssey from Greenland to Africa, and if a wheatear could consciously make risk assessments, surely it makes sense for a land bird to avoid crossing the North Atlantic?

These are questions almost unanswerable in 1960, but fifty years' of research, using increasingly sophisticated science, has given some clues to help us solve these puzzles. Migrants like wheatears use as cues for navigation the stars, the position of the sun, and can sense the Earth's magnetic fields. Take away night guides such as the stars with the onset of rain and fog, and unfavourable winds, and many birds become confused and disorientated.

Because wheatears spread out from Africa, they are 'programmed' to return there to winter, where habitat and food supplies are guaranteed amenable compared to the harsh northern winters. Flight directions and timings are internally controlled and evolutionary changes that may influence these occur in small steps. For Greenland birds, or those of Siberia, to choose shorter routes to different wintering grounds would require major directional shifts for the migratory flights. Small changes would means birds ending up in the Pacific Ocean or the South Atlantic. So they stick to what they know and fly, and fly, and many arrive to winter in Africa and return north when something triggers a departure again: determined birds, amazing journeys.

Rathlin Bird Observatory 1960-1961

A bird observatory is a place with well defined boundaries where birds, in particular migrating birds, are observed and studied by resident and visiting enthusiasts.

In the 1960s, interest in bird migration was boosted by field workers who manned a chain of observatories around the coasts of Britain and Ireland and on offshore islands. There was an already long-established bird observatory at Copeland Islands off the north County Down coast, and another was running for several years in the late 1950s and 1960s at Tory Island off north-west County Donegal, so Rathlin was well placed between these two to compare observations. At various periods within the early 1960s observers carried out watches at Inishtrahull Island off north Donegal, the Maidens' Islands lighthouse off east County Antrim and at St. John's Point lighthouse in south County Down.

The base for the Rathlin Bird Observatory of 1960-1961 was, as mentioned above, the East Lighthouse at Altacarry Head. The resident lighthouse keepers here gave us their full cooperation, alerting us to weather forecasts and allowing access to the lighthouse tower and lantern platform.

The north-south arm of the island (East Lighthouse to Rue Point) was covered daily by observers from 20 August to 27 September 1960, and from 10 April to 25 May, and 1 September to 3 October in 1961, with additional observations by two visitors from 2 to 11 August 1961. The manning of such a bird observatory is hard physical work; you must visit all of the suitable terrestrial habitats each day to record birds present, carry out watches from vantage points to log seabird movements, visit the lighthouse lantern area on nights when migrating birds are flying about the light and carry out trapping (at Rathlin mainly with mist nets in various habitats) to ring and examine migrants.

Fifteen individuals helped man the observatory in 1960 but only six (plus the visiting two in August) were available in 1961. The driving force behind setting up and supervising the running of Rathlin Bird Observatory was two dedicated ornithologists – Tom Ennis of County Down and Tony Tree of the then Rhodesia in Africa. Tony manned the observatory single-handed for long periods in 1961.

The observatory's daily logbook records a total of 129 species of birds for the above periods in 1960-1961, including several rarities the highlight of which was Northern Ireland's first record of a wryneck, a member of the woodpecker family (a little smaller than a starling and with grey and rufous plumage and an owl-like ability to twist its head through almost 360 degrees). It was caught at the lighthouse on the night of 30 August 1960, ringed and released. As soon as we let it go the next morning, it flew to the roughcast wall of the lighthouse and clung on vertically, in woodpecker style, before flying off to continue its journey.

In 1960, 118 birds of 22 species were trapped by mist net and 18 birds of 7 species were caught at the light, all of which were ringed. In 1961, 381 birds of 32 species were caught and ringed (238 mist netted, 49 at the light, 75 as nestlings and 19 by hand). Annual Reports were produced; Rathlin Bird Observatory 1960, and in 1961 the report included studies at the Maidens lighthouse and Saint John's Point lighthouse. This Rathlin work put on record many valuable observations and made useful contributions to the study of bird migration in the early 1960s.

We found the island to be a rewarding place to study bird migration, but it is so large that it was impossible to cover all of it in search of migrants . Even while concentrating only on the southern arm we had difficulty maintaining the work and after two years it was abandoned as a bird observatory.

Sea Passage

Sitting in the narrow channel between Scotland and Ireland yet facing the Atlantic western approaches to Britain, Rathlin is like a traffic island in a stream of migrating seabirds. Shearwaters, skuas, petrels, kittiwakes and other oceanic species move ahead of the autumnal low pressure systems sweeping across the Atlantic Ocean from Newfoundland and further south. In strong westerly winds, they come up against the coast of Scotland and some move into the northern part of the Irish Sea. As each depression passes, and winds veer to the north-west, many of these birds navigate back to the Atlantic by coasting – that is, they follow the coastlines, passing close to islands and mainland promontories such as Ramore Head at Portrush and Malin Head in north Donegal. Rathlin is well situated to intercept such traffic, and we huddle on vantage points such as Altacarry Head and Rue Point and watch these ocean travellers fly past. On less stormy days, we note seabirds passing on their way to feeding grounds, or gathering offshore when shoals of fish are located and the birds are plunging and diving for food. These flocks include gulls and terns and many of the auks (guillemots, razorbills and puffins) that breed on cliffs of islands such as Rathlin and the Hebrides. They are joined by high diving gannets, many no doubt from their nearby summer breeding site on the great granite lump of Ailsa Craig off Scotland's Ayrshire coast. By August most of these birds have finished breeding for the current year and are stocking up on food and laying down fat reserves to see them through an energy-draining moult and their long migrations and a winter at sea.

Storm-bound on Rathlin fifty years later, in September 2010, I sit at Rue Point hugging the shelter of the lighthouse and watch kittiwakes, gannets, small petrels, skuas and shearwaters beat past into a severe gale shrieking in from the west. Green water crashes over the rocks, spray wets me and some of the gannets pass so close I can see them scan the sea's surface, head tilted slightly down – these big strong birds, heading for the Bay of Biscay, are keeping a look out for a fish. Now and then one dives, dropping like a stone into the sea, wings thrown back at the last moment. They have left behind their young at the breeding colonies, living off their fat reserves and soon to make their own way west and south down the coasts of Britain and Ireland. Four days later, during a very bumpy ferry crossing to the mainland, I spot one of this year's juvenile gannets in its distinctive sooty black plumage beating west into the wind, finding its own way to a fish-rich wintering area, perhaps off Morocco and northwest Africa.

2. DROPPING A LINE

Rathlin's Sea Fisheries

"Fish did you say? Ah, sure, there's no fish now compared to when I was a youngster. You could hardly get a line to the sea bed the mackerel and herring shoals were that thick."

Over almost a lifetime of field work, I've heard similar comments, be they about the shoals of herring, or the great numbers of game on shoots of long ago in the Antrim hills, or how the corncrakes would keep you awake at nights so many were there calling in the Donegal hay meadows. Such tales of 'the good old days' could be dismissed as nostalgia mixed with a bit of exaggeration were it not for the sad fact that there's more truth in these 'if only you'd been here then...' stories than you might credit from the expansive language of the tellers. I've been around long enough to have experienced corncrakes in abundance, lots of snipe and hares in the bogs and fields and yes, big catches of fish; certainly at Rathlin more fish than seem to be about now . In terms of Irish sea whitefish and coastal lobsters and crabs I have the notebooks and published papers to prove the point. As for the 'big shoots', gamekeepers' logbooks and estate records often confirm the bags. Much of the remaining information on past numbers and diversity of our fish and other wildlife is fading as older generation observers join their deceased relatives, while some of their stories have entered the folklore of coast and country regions. Thus it's important, I believe, to mine what's left of this resource of memories, sift the twinkle in the eye stuff to fit into an appropriate story, distil the essence and not leave this lying in dust-gathering notebooks.

Archaeological excavations at Mesolithic and Neolithic sites demonstrate that fish have been part of our diet for our entire occupation of the island of Ireland, going back almost ten thousand years. Depending on where you lived, it varied in importance. Not surprisingly, on inhabited islands fish was a major part of diet and, in many cases, important to the local economy. However, the tricky part was catching them.

This is not about angling; it's concerned with sea fishing for food rather than sport, and to make a living from commercial fishing. Rathlin has quite a good harbour now, certainly good enough to be a bit overcrowded at times. Nevertheless, like most north Antrim ports, it supports – ferries excluded – mainly small vessels. In the past, tiny piers and remote coves around the island sheltered a few fishing boats but today most of these places are long abandoned.

Sudden changes in the weather from calm to battering gales, powerful tidal streams and currents, areas of very deep water, a largely cliff-bound coast – all these contribute to make fishing around Rathlin a risky occupation. Detailed knowledge of weather signs, sea conditions, the habits of fish, land marks for locating fishing grounds (called *Meiths* in North Antrim), a great deal of caution and some superstition (see Folklore) combine to make the Rathliners skilled fishermen. Fish was a greater part of the diet and economy of the island in the past, when both physical and financial access to outside supplies was limited.

The geologist and naturalist Reverend William Hamilton, on Rathlin briefly in August 1784, did not mention fish; it was Dr J.D.

Marshall, secretary to the Natural History Society of Belfast, who gave some detail of fish and fishing after he visited Rathlin in the 1830s. He acknowledged Mrs Catherine Gage of the island's landlord family as supplying a lot of information and a combination of Marshall's 1837 account and Mrs Gage's 1851 history of the island gives an idea of Rathlin's sea fisheries in the 19th century.

Today we are used to hearing of the scarcity of cod and how much it is over-fished, so it is interesting to note that Marshall, paraphrasing Mrs Gage, said this fish was formerly very abundant at Rathlin but by the time of his visit cod was only occasionally caught. The fishes that formed the largest catches around the island were coalfish (known locally as *glashan*), pollack (*lythe*), grey gurnard and, usually caught from the rocks around the shores, wrasse, called *morans* or *mearn* on Rathlin, pronounced 'murrans', as used hereafter. Both line fishing and nets were employed in the catching. Other species were taken in variable numbers, some for food and some for bait for lines and lobster and crab creels. Marshall and Gage listed skate, plaice, sole, turbot, bream, dogfish and ling, and comment that both lobster and common crab (probably the edible or brown crab) were also sought. Herring was not mentioned by Gage in 1851 (but it is by earlier members of this family) while Marshall suggested that the strong tides around Rathlin kept these fish away. Mackerel, according to Gage, were seldom taken, but it's not clear if this means they were there but not sought or were absent. Both authors say how abundant were sand eels – they called them *launce* – and how they provided important food for the seabirds. The glashans were valuable not only for food but for the oil in their livers which was used for lamps on the island. Fish were dried and salted for use over winter and murrans especially were preserved by these methods.

Marshall noted that "common crab or *partin...* are very abundant around all the shores [of the island] and are sought after by boys for bait to the wrasse or murran." At nearby Dunseverick, across the sound from Rathlin, crabs were taken in considerable numbers in the first four decades of the 20th century, with interruptions to the fisheries by two world wars. The average open fishing boat would work two to four dozen pots and creels, taking four to eight barrels of crabs (120 lbs, 55 kg of crab to a barrel) in a good week over the spring and summer. In each barrel the crabs were packed with damp seaweed to keep them cool and moist and were collected by buyers twice a week and sent to Liverpool. Occasionally local fishing boats would intercept cargo vessels bound for English ports and transfer their catches directly; a dangerous manoeuvre. Lobster fishing in those days was over a short summer period, usually July and August, and long line fishing for various whitefish and flatfish was a major occupation throughout the year.

Michael Murphy, on Rathlin in 1953 and 1954 to collect folklore, gave snippets of information on fishing, quoting material gathered from both younger fishermen and from the memories of older residents and going back probably to the early part of the 20th century (*Murphy 1987*). He recorded that Rathliners could never cure mackerel because they were too oily and were given tips on how to do this by a mainland fisherman. This surprises me, so I assume mackerel were being caught in the mid 1950s but were probably eaten fresh and almost certainly used to bait creels and lines. Both mackerel and herring used to be abundant around Rathlin and we caught both species there in the 1970s.

Around the turn of the century (19th/20th), north Antrim coast fishermen came to the island for a few days a week to fish with lines and creels and stayed overnight in some of the caves. They travelled over from small ports such as Dunseverick on the Antrim mainland on a Sunday but did not fish on the Sabbath. The creels and pots were fished Monday to Wednesday then the catch was brought home for market and they returned to the island to fish till Saturday.

Islander Alex Morrison in his memoir (2003) gave an account of draught net fishing from around the 1920s to the Second World War. He said nothing about the species caught but described how the nets were set by boat and hauled in from the land by teams of fishermen. It was common for a number of men to have shares in a boat's ownership and its catches. The draught netting activities were carried out close to known spots for certain fish and the caves along the southern shores of the western arm of the island were used to store gear and for shelter and brewing up tea.

By the time I arrived on Rathlin to study fisheries (1970-75), fishing was dependent mainly on lobster, with a by-catch of brown crabs. Glashan and lythe were still popular and available, morans too, and herring and mackerel varied in abundance and were sometimes taken in good quantities. Today (2010) brown crabs are fished along with lobsters, but there is only one full-time fishing boat operating from Rathlin, catching lobsters and crabs and fish when available, and the two-man crew's main problem is bait supply – catching bait fish around the island is proving unreliable and demanding in time and bait often has to be bought in from Co. Down fishing ports, an added expense involving the effort to travel to collect it. With quotas and other restrictions being applied, not many sea fishing vessels now land damaged or unwanted fish that may be suitable for bait. A few small island boats fish lobster and crab and also jig and troll lines for fish, activities shared with farming and other work. Vessels from elsewhere fish around Rathlin at times, taking lobster, crab and scallops.

Nippers and Creepers

Like bad drivers, lobsters and crabs have a tendency to back into things. On the deck of a fishing boat when shaken out of a creel they will scrabble backwards and, in the case of crabs, sideways as well, making for the nearest dark corner and only settling when they feel something secure at their back. Then they face this strange new water-less world, antennae twitching and formidable claws at the ready. Underwater, at home, they are found lurking under boulders or in crevices, the vulnerable back end jammed into safety, the heavy armoury presented to whatever dares to approach. Through long experience, fishermen handle them with care. Twice, a large crab snapped one of my fingers – the same one each time. That unfortunate digit now has a permanent kink, a souvenir of shaking hands with 2 kilogram (4.5 pounds) north Antrim crabs and a reminder of moments of carelessness in handling these formidable creatures.

I've had many happy days out with Rathlin's lobster fishermen and the following is typical. We set off early in the morning in the *Golden Dawn,* an 8 metre (26 ft) open fishing boat, heading west close to the cliff columns of vivid white chalk that looked like great teeth bared in a smile. We pause to lift a line of creels near the Dutchman's Leg. The Rathlin fishermen have names for much of their coast rarely seen from land and thus many were not known to the terrestrially confined map makers. The water this morning is a very pale blue and a slight ripple of thousands of wavering lenses reflect a jigsaw of the white cliffs. Kelp beds show up at a distance as a purple stain in the water then, close up you see the canopy of brown fronds waving below the boat. Beams of sunlight splay out in the green depths and catch the snow of plankton (tiny free-floating plants and animals of the sea) drifting past on the tide. Occasionally, little comb jellies – known as sea gooseberries – jerk by, their transparent bodies catching the light and splitting it into a rainbow of colours.

Amongst all this life floating, drifting, pulsating and flagellating below us will be thousands of the spiky, weird-looking transparent larvae of lobsters and crabs, a few evading predators long enough to become adults, and hopefully some of those we will tempt into our creels, laid on the sea bed with their reeking bait.

We re-set the creels off the white cliffs, having thrown overboard many small edible crabs that were too small to keep, and retain one medium sized lobster, which now has rubber bands binding its two large claws together so it won't damage others when put in the storage box later. Then we move on to the north-west of the island where underwater cliffs drop 200 metres (over 600 ft) just a short distance off shore. In these depths where it is constantly cold and dark, we have laid several lines of pots and creels. Pots tend to have a single entrance at the top, or one at each end on the wooden-slatted and cylindrical barrel pot, while creels are cottage-shaped, usually with side entrances. The general term 'traps' refers to any baited construction that will catch lobsters and crabs and prawns. The word is used little on this side of the Atlantic, being more common to USA lobster men.

This year (1971), the crew of the *Golden Dawn* pioneered lobster fishing in deep water. It takes a tremendous length of rope to drop traps so far, for you have to allow much more than the actual depth to cope with currents and tides pulling at the line of creels. We begin the slow haul to the surface of a set of six. The small winch on the boat groans as the combined weight of rope and creels strain it to capacity. I wait with muted excitement, for this is the first time I've been on board for a lift from such deep water , and we all wonder – for nobody can be sure – what will come up in the creels. I know there is a terrific pressure down there, and yet everything that reaches the surface seems lively. In the second creel is a large lobster, at least two kilograms (4.5 pounds) weight and about half a metre (over 1.5 ft) in length. She is not the dark blue-black of normal-sized inshore lobsters, but has a bluish-pink colouration, quite spotted in places. We handle her carefully, banding the massive claws and laying her gently in a box with seaweed over her. The temperature change from the depths to the surface puts a strain on these lobsters and they need to be kept cool. The rest of the day's deep water fishing produces a dozen large lobsters and several big edible crabs. The crabs are both males and females, but ten of the twelve lobsters are females. The smaller lobsters we return to the sea, watching as they sink slowly out of sight, although some engage their rapid escape response, which is a powerful flap of the abdomen and tail, which pulls them rapidly through the water, backwards to safety. I wonder briefly if lobsters feel relief.

In September 1972 we tagged, marked and released 339 lobsters around Rathlin. By April 1973 we had recaptured 32 of these marked animals (9%), and all but two had remained close to the island. Of the stay-at-homes, 22 had moved less than 1 km (0.8 miles), 8 had strayed between 1-9 kms (0.8 – 5.5 miles) and the the two wanderers had reached Dunseverick on the nearby mainland, a journey of just over 10 kms (6 miles). Some of the marked lobsters were caught more than once.

The crew who helped me catch, mark and release these lobsters fish for a living and we have an agreement, supplemented by cash, that any marketable-sized lobsters marked or carrying a tag will be returned to the sea. My attempt to trace lobster movements around the island are met with a mixture of helpful hints, cooperation and some wry amusement by the island's fishermen. Having paid out five times for one particular tagged lobster over the summer, I suggest:

"Are you keeping this beast in a secret pot somewhere and selling it to me over and over?"

"Would we do that to you?" comes the hurt reply, but I see the twinkle in the eyes. "It's a trap-happy lobster. You find some like that now and then, maybe an under-sized one with distinctive markings you get to know and of course it eventually grows big enough to keep, and that's the end of it."

Well, yes, quite feasible, considering our recaptures - they certainly weren't trap-shy. That's their downfall. I often think how determined these spiky creatures are in their clamber across the netting of the creels and in through one, maybe two, entrance funnels to the parlour end of the trap to get to a piece of salted and stinking fish that they have to pull to pieces while keeping at bay hungry crabs already present. If I had to go to so much trouble for my fish supper I'd probably change my diet.

The Rathlin lobster tagging experiment showed what the fishermen already suspected: that the island's lobster resource was a resident population and therefore particularly susceptible to over-fishing. Further research we carried out offshore in September 1973 showed that there were larger, older lobsters living in suitable habitat at some rocky pinnacles and areas of rough seabed. Many of these were big egg-bearing females and were likely to have been important providers of young lobsters to the north coast fisheries. These sites and others are now fished for lobsters regularly, and the protection of egg-bearing females is helped by punching a V-notch in the tail and releasing them. It is now prohibited to take such marked lobsters.

Lobsters are now a luxury item and choosing one at a restaurant will set you back quite a packet of cash and even then you'll probably be served half-a-lobster. If you are eating in a modern European city the creature has probably travelled expensively to reach your plate, and many north Antrim lobsters end up in Paris. Such a perishable food item – lobsters have to be marketed alive – travels by air and usually passes from the fisherman's hands to a dealer to a deliverer to a chef to a waiter and hence to your plate and the cost accumulates with each stage. In Victorian times, seafood was abundant and lobsters and oysters, to name but two luxury seafoods today, were fed to the masses and there were clauses in employment contracts to stipulate that such foods would not be offered to employees more than twice a week.

The history of marine fisheries and their exploitation is filled with accounts of super abundance to scarcity as fish and shellfish have been reduced by increasingly efficient fishing operations and the prices have rocketed accordingly. Cod is now often more expensive than the best steak or shellfish and features in the costly section of menus. The supermarkets are now filled with more reasonably priced former luxuries such as salmon and prawns, many 'farmed' in enclosures in the sea and estuaries, although reading the packaging labels might surprise you in terms of origins.

Compared with luxury seafoods, brown crabs never seem to have caught up with their upper-crust neighbours: the lobsters, langoustines and crawfish. While lobsters are valuable enough to fly to far-off destinations, crabs seem to be eaten nearer home. They are, for their sizes, heavy animals and lower prices always inhibited transport to distant markets. Processors helped by purchasing locally-caught crabs and extracting, cooking and freezing the flesh so that only the edible bits were transported. In the past decade or so, demand for small species of crabs such as the velvet swimming crab has increased and around Northern Ireland these are now taken in fair quantities, but at Rathlin, it is only the brown crab that is marketed. Back in the 1970s, we threw most of these overboard or kept some for bait or to eat at home. A few mainland coast fishermen had outlets through fishmongers for some brown crabs, but the trade was local and small.

About Lobsters

When you see a lobster out of the water, as most of us do unless we are sub-aqua divers, sitting on a fish-monger's slab or in a box by a quayside, it is an awkward, spiky and quite weird looking creature. American east coast fishermen call them 'bugs'. There *is* something a bit cockroach-like about them, which is not surprising as both are arthropods - animals with hard segmented bodies and limbs.

Lobsters and crabs are crustaceans, which I always think is a good word for such creatures, for they are crusty in structure and by nature. However, drop a live lobster back into the sea or encounter one in a deep rock pool and you immediately see how well adapted it is to underwater life. Released from a boat into the water, or startled in the pool or on the seabed, with a few flicks of its muscular abdomen and broad tail it shoots off backwards at speed. It pays to get out of its way under these circumstances, for it has no wing mirrors and can scatter fish or anything else in its way. When undisturbed, lobsters blunder about in forward gear like well armoured tanks, using the long and hyper-sensitive antennae to detect any vibrations in the water that might signal food, or danger. They also have a highly developed sense of smell and reasonable eyesight in dim light. Food comprises almost anything they can lay their claws on, including live prey and dead flesh. They are not, for all their high culinary reputation, fussy eaters and if you enjoy lobster flesh then don't enquire too closely into *their* diet.

Recent research on the North American lobster, very similar to our European one, has revealed amazing details of their private lives. Here are a few examples:

Lobsters pee through their heads. The head region contains two sizeable urine bladders and the creatures can force a jet of urine out into the sea through nozzles close to the small forward attenules. Lobster urine contains chemicals that seem to enable lobsters to recognise each other. By peeing in each other's faces – whether in a fight or in a pre-mating ritual – it's likely they are emitting specific chemical signatures.

Lobsters develop a detailed knowledge of their home ground; who's occupying which hole or crevice; where empty shelters are; where the nearest hiding place lies if danger threatens.

They start life with both claws the same but by favouring one for crushing and the other for slicing the claws become asymmetrical – a bulky crusher with slow-operating muscle and a sharp slicer with fast-operating muscle, of the type in the abdomen and tail region that produces the quick-flip escape reaction. These claws are formidable weapons in a fight and equally matched lobsters can inflict serious and even lethal damage on each other. It pays to back off when threatened rather than engage, especially when the opponent is larger.

It has long been known that the larval stages of lobsters float free in the ocean currents before they moult into miniature adult form and settle on the sea bed for the rest of their lives. Recent studies have shown that for a short time, a matter of a week or two, the miniature adults, before they settle, can swim in a forward motion using the tiny swimmerets, like paddles, on their underparts. They are aided in this motion by keeping their claws held forward, close together, to give a more streamlined shape like a human performing a high dive. In such a way they could it has been calculated, swim up to 1.5 km (1 mile) per day. That gives them a little control over where they finally settle. The ideal settling place is a sea bed covered with cobbles, which are medium-sized rounded stones that provide shelter and areas to search for food.

Lobster Love Life

"Do you know how lobsters have sex?" a fisherman asked me one day while we sat, the engine idling, waiting for the tide to slacken so that we could life some pots. "Carefully, I imagine" was my reply. "No, really, do you know?" he insisted. "Yes" I said, and waited for him to probe further. "Me too," he responded, then he set to, lifting the pots. We never discussed lobster love life again, and I still wonder if we had the same knowledge, or did he know something smutty that had escaped me.

Most crustaceans carry the burden of having to cast their entire shell, called moulting, in order to grow. It's a complete change of outer clothes, like us stripping off hat, coat, gloves, shoes and socks. In lobsters, underneath is a newly forming shell which expands as the creature takes in water. Until this hardens, a freshly moulted animal is very vulnerable to attack. It is at this traumatic stage that the female lobster mates, having released a chemical love letter called a pheromone which is picked up by the male. It may sound like soft porn, but what happens next is the hard and spiky male couples with the soft and vulnerable female and he inserts a sperm package which she retains under her abdomen. Then he's off, job done, and she carries the love present for several months, the duration depending on when mating took place –

early summer and she fertilises her eggs about September, late summer and she carries the sperm till spring. When ready to lay, she turns on her back and extrudes the eggs, passing them over the male's gift so that they are fertilised, then attaches them to sticky feathery appendages on her underside so that the lower half of her body carries all these green eggs. Depending on the female's size, each individual can carry from ten thousand to over fifty thousand eggs. When it comes to putting all your eggs in one basket, the female lobster takes this old cliché to extremes. Lobsters like lots of babies for a good reason. After the eggs hatch and the larvae are set free to take their chance in the open ocean, only a fraction of one percent survive to become adults, the rest eaten by predators while in the floating plankton or being guzzled by fish and other hungry creatures when the lobsterlings settle on the sea bed. Once they are big enough to venture further afield, they discover baited lobster pots and we are added to their list of enemies.

More Than a Blush

As everyone who has eaten lobster knows, they are red. Those who have seen a live one will also know that their natural colour is a dark blue. So why the colour change on cooking? Lobster colouring is chemically complex and on occasions live red ones turn up, also various shades of blue from pale through cobalt to the normal inky blue, some with shades of pink mixed in and even green and yellow lobsters exist. They can be spotted, marbled and otherwise patterned. Are they like an octopus that can change its colour quickly to match its environment? Not quite, but environment matters in terms of colour, related to diet, type of sea bed and the amount of sunlight that reaches them, so depth also comes into the equation. Blue to red on cooking happens because most lobsters obtain carotenoid substances in their diet, which are what gives carrots their colour. In lobsters the carotenoid pigment formed is known as *astaxanthin*. This binds to proteins in the lobster's shell to make it blue, and cooking destroys this bonding and releases the carotenoids to produce orange-red. Other crustaceans go red or pinkish on cooking, notably grey prawns and shrimps. The Norway lobster or Dublin Bay prawn, the much loved scampi, is already bright orange in life. Colourful characters, these marine crustaceans, physically and in temperament.

Other Spiky Critters

Out with the fishermen, and also pottering about Rathlin's stony and rocky shores, I've come across other shellfish that would make a knight of old in full battle dress look like a wimp. The sea bed swarms with nippers and creepers. One of my favourites is the crawfish, also known as the spiny lobster. It has no large front claws but makes up for this by being liberally covered with spikes, sharp as any hypodermic needle. Crawfish are of a similar range of sizes to a lobster but they are highly coloured. The entire body shell is brownish-purple with orange and yellow legs and pale orange *uropods*, the five broad tail segments that can be spread like an oriental fan. The two large antennae at the front have spines on the first few segments, the whole carapace is covered with small forward-projecting spikes and the abdomen to the tail has vicious backward-facing razor-like projections. The crawfish's abdomen and tail end is the part we like to eat, delicious sweet meat. It is an expensive meal and one familiar to those prepared to pay for it on Mediterranean holidays. The crawfish prefers somewhat warmer waters than lobsters, although it can tolerate cool seas and small numbers inhabit the deep crevices on underwater cliffs on Rathlin's western and northern sides. Here we caught occasional crawfish using the cylindrical wooden-slatted barrel pot, with a wide top entrance. This is the favoured gear for catching these creatures, although in some areas fishermen set a tangle or trammel net for them.

Not so spiky, but the overall winner for grumpiness, is the small velvet swimming crab. It may have a velvety feel to its carapace but there's nothing else soft about this denizen of rock pools and inshore waters. Lifting pots around Rathlin, we would dread a catch of velvets. They are a greyish brown colour with blue stripes and bright red eyes. They act as if the red eyes denote a permanent hangover. Very agile, as soon as you put a hand into the pot, the claws are up in a threat. They can draw blood, so sharp are these weapons. Aggressive, agile, fast hit-and-run warriors with superior armaments, velvets would be natural candidates if there were an SAS regiment for crabs. We used to throw them overboard as fast as possible, but now they are a valuable species, actively fished for the European sea-food markets.

Moving north from the Mediterranean and southern Britain is the spiny spider crab, whose smaller relative the spider crab occurs around our coasts. All this sharpness starts early – the free-floating larval stages of lobsters and crabs, hatched from eggs and living for a few weeks in the plankton, are transparent and fragile but usually with one or more spines sticking out somewhere. Alien-looking creatures, they eventually go through several moults and gradually come to resemble miniature adults, by which point they settle on the sea bed.

3. WHERE THE STONES SPEAK

There is a poem from the island that says if you tell your troubles to the same stone long enough it will speak to you. Our history on this planet is a mere blink in time compared with even the most 'recent' rocks, so if the stones speak, be prepared to listen to a long story.

The Drowned Magpie

It was the pied appearance of Rathlin's chalk and basalt cliffs rising out of the sea that prompted Charles Kingsley to have his character Cary christen the island 'the drowned magpie' in the historical novel *Westward Ho!* First published in 1855, the book is set in the reign of Elizabeth the First. After a long conflict with the McDonnells of Antrim, Elizabeth I ceded Rathlin to Angus McDonnell in 1585 and began to gather her ships and other forces for defence against the Armada threat. The chapter from which the quote is taken (chapter XXXII) describes how the surviving Spanish Armada ships are fleeing in 1588 down the west coast of Scotland and around the Irish coast.

Rathlin sits at a busy marine crossroads. Strong tides and currents mix Atlantic, North Channel and Irish Sea waters, and its nearest island neighbours are Scottish – Islay, Jura and Gigha – while the Scottish mainland at the Mull of Kintyre is visible on clear days just across the channel. For thousands of years marine trade has linked the island to Scotland and much further afield. So where does Rathlin belong? Is it the most southerly island of the Hebridean archipelago or is it a part of Ireland? You do not need to be a geologist to realise that Rathlin is a cut-out of the north County Antrim mainland. From any high point on the island the view across to the Causeway Coast's blackish basalts and white chalk gives a very similar pattern to Rathlin as seen from the mainland. Culturally the island has many links with Scotland but geologically it belongs to Northern Ireland. The dark basalts of Rathlin have the same volcanic origin as those of the Giant's Causeway and the Causeway Coast.

If the 'drowned magpie' appearance is not enough evidence, then consider the island's creation myth. Finn MacCool, legendary colossus who built the nearby Giant's Causeway, found this a thirsty job and he drank Ireland dry of whiskey. He sent his mother – also of substantial build - to Scotland to replenish supplies. She filled her apron with local rocks – black basalt and white chalk – to use as stepping stones but before she had gone far her apron split and the stones fell into the Sea of Moyle to give us Rathlin Island.

Much of the island sits on a bed of chalk but it is only on the south side of the western arm that this white rock rises to present cliff faces topped with dark basalt, like ice cream with a thick layer of chocolate sauce. Elsewhere around Rathlin's shores the chalk is either dropped deep below the sea by faults or exposed only as shore platforms or raised beaches. Basalt dominates the island and if you approach Rathlin by sea from the west or north it presents a daunting profile of dark and sombre cliffs up to 120 metres (almost 400 ft) in height.

Rathliners still sometimes say Ireland is an island just south of Rathlin! In the 'old days' it was considered a severe punishment to be banished to Ireland. Look at Rathlin from the high summit of nearby

Fair Head and you see an L-shaped island with its two arms reaching out to embrace Ireland. Rathlin knows where it belongs.

Geology and Scenery

The two arms of this angular island are scenically quite different. The three lighthouses make useful reference points. The western arm, from the East Light near Altacarry Head to the West Light at Tieveleog in Kebble townland, contains most of the high ground with considerable areas over 100 m (over 330 ft). Basalt escarpments slant across the island with valleys between, created by different lava flows, erosion and faulting. From the East Light to Rue Point lighthouse, the southern arm is less hilly, although not without some significant cliffs on the west side and with a much indented lower shore facing east. The low-lying sweep of Church Bay is different again, made up of chalk raised beach and platforms and containing numerous fields and settlements. At times of higher sea level – about 30 m (nearly 100 ft) above present – this lower lying land was subject to scouring by the ocean which must have almost divided Rathlin in two. Islanders used to say that there were 'two Ragheries' and I was shown, from a boat off the east coast, an area where you could see across the island to the sound on the other side.

A retreating ice sheet around twelve thousand years ago left Rathlin scraped clean and pitted with rocky hollows now obvious as numerous small lakes. Glacial drift – gravels and sand – is thin on the island although there are hollows with accumulated soils that were recognised as fertile and settled and farmed over many generations. There are a few red and blue clay deposits.

Exploring the Chalk

Geologists discuss millions of years the way we chat about last week. Basalt is 'recent', chalk is a bit older and to get to a word such as 'ancient' you have to think in billions of years. The two tiny islands of Inishtrahull, west of Rathlin off the north tip of County Donegal, are 1.8 billion years old. That's heading towards ancient. Anyway, they don't belong in this book and it's doubtful if they belong to Ireland in geological terms – they're more akin to parts of the Hebrides or even Greenland.

About 90 million years ago, in the Cretaceous Period (*creta* is Latin for chalk) warm seas covered much of what is now Western Europe, sea levels then being 200 metres (650 feet) higher than now. By 75 million years ago, Ireland's chalk was being laid down in a warm sea such as above that pulsated with life. A lot of this life – really a lot – was comprised of tiny algae called *coccolithophores* which produce *calcite* (chalk) to form *coccoliths* inside their cells. Ten million of the smallest coccolithophores laid end to end would extend to only one metre. These algae are still about, sometimes swept together by ocean gyres to turn the Atlantic milky, and the constant snowfall of dead shells to the seabed builds up lime-rich oozes which pressure and time transform into layers of the rock we know as white limestone or chalk.

What's left of the chalk in Ireland is now largely confined to County Antrim (there is a small outcrop in south-west Ireland) and much of it is dropped far out of our sight by faulting or buried under great coatings of basalt following volcanic outpourings which we'll come to soon. The bits left add much to the Antrim coast scenery. Around Rathlin's white cliffs and shores, three interesting features of the chalk, apart from its obvious scenic qualities, are the caves, the bands of hard flints and the fossils. Viewed from the sea, Rathlin's chalk cliffs from Lacknakilly just west of the harbour stretch over three kilometres (almost two miles) to west of Cooraghy Bay and are like great white teeth pitted with dark cavities which, as you approach closer, are seen to be caves. Many of these caves are now above sea level on exposed rock platforms, but were originally cut into vertical fractures in the chalk by a sea that was at a higher level than now. At the western end of the chalk cliffs some of the caves are quite high up and in places there are deep crevices and tunnels. Inside the caves, water trickles and drips and where light penetrates the cave walls and floors are green with mosses, algae and liverworts. Most caves quickly become narrow and some are very shallow.

The chalk cliffs are studded with horizontal bands of brown flints (a kind of crystalline silica) and elsewhere larger flint nodules occur. Many flint tools and weapons from the Mesolithic and Neolithic periods have been found around the Antrim coast and nearby sites, including Rathlin.

Parts of the island's shoreline are comprised of chalk. There are extensive bedrock exposures in Church Bay and Mill Bay that are pitted and shelved and thus good rock-pool areas. Below the high cliffs at the western end of the long bay known as Altahuile on the north side of Rathlin is a shelf of fantastically eroded chalk, with ragged pinnacles and gullies. This is a difficult place to get to but worth the effort just to see what wave action can do to the chalk. On the south arm of the island from Inandrian to Portantoonish – accessible by a grassy scramble down between headlands – is a shore made up of chalk platforms which contains huge rolled flints, many black rather than the usual rich brown. Elsewhere, in some bays and coves, you will find a salt-and-pepper pattern of chalk and basalt stones, cobbles and boulders.

An ancient natural history is written in this vivid white chalk. Fossils of sponges, squid-like creatures, ammonites (nautilus-like animals that lived in coiled shells), sea urchins and others occur in the various layers of the chalk cliffs and bedrocks along the shores, a record of life in the seas of the later Cretaceous period (80-65 million years ago). This story can be read and interpreted by geologists and those of related disciplines, but with a magnifying lens and a good guide to fossils, especially micro-fossils, you can surprise yourself by finding the remains of amazing creatures.

In the evening sun, if you sit outside the pub or a bit further south with a view across Church Bay, the chalk cliffs from Lacknakilly to Sroanlea are thrown into strong relief by light and shadows. The ridges and furrows of the grassy tops end in precipitous columns that give an illusion of tall gables. It is an extraordinary sight as the setting sun turns the chalk pink, then all fall into shadow as the sun sinks out of sight over the island's western arm.

Braving the Basalt

Rock climbers will tell you to watch out for the basalt. It is a variable rock in terms of structure – seemingly hard until you are close and find it much fractured both vertically and horizontally, and sections can come away in your hand. There are layers of slaggy, crumbly rock and slopes of variable sized fallen stones known as scree. Climbers prefer to brave the dolerite, a type of basalt that was intruded into existing lava flows, forced up from underground and forming a much harder rock, best seen on the huge cliffs of Fair Head that shine in the evening sun across the sound from Rue Point on Rathlin.

The County Antrim basalts are thus of three types: those that were extruded from cracks, vents and volcanoes covering large areas; some of a type that cooled to give columns; and the intruded lavas cooling slowly to produce hard dolerite as described above.

Although the island presents a black and white face to us on the mainland, you have to get closer to see any colour. Grey and green algae and general weathering can mark the chalk in places, and millions of years ago, during tropical climatic periods with wet and dry seasons, the basalts weathered to crumbly rock and soils that are red, purple, orange, yellow and brown, revealing layers known as *lithomarge* and *laterite* and containing silica and ores of iron and aluminium (*bauxite*). These colours are most obvious in the inter-basaltic beds, which are crumbly layers between two major basalt types, the lower basalts and the *tholeitic* basalts which tend to be the ones with the best examples of columns similar to those that make the Giant's Causeway so famous. However, there are large areas of the basalt cliff faces, especially at the western and north-western end, where reddish weathering or part-weathering is very obvious. This is notable particularly at Derginan Point – in Irish *An Deargán*, 'the red place'. You can find quite small but equally colourful exposures in the basalts at many places around the island.

Ring of fire

Although the chalk is very obvious, it is basalt that dominates the island. Basalt is a common type of rock throughout the world. It is an igneous rock formed when lava cools. In the North Atlantic 'ring of fire', there are *igneous provinces*, as they are known, occurring in Greenland, northwest Scotland and northeast Ireland, originating in an Icelandic hot-spot. The basalts of County Antrim, including those of Rathlin, are between 60 and 55 million years old, and most were extruded from long cracks or fissures, and from former volcanoes such as Slemish Mountain in mid-Antrim being a prominent example, now plugged with hard rock.

This ring of fire left massive amounts of basalt which have gradually, through erosion by ice, water, wind and chemicals, formed distinctive landscapes, some of spectacular form like the Giant's Causeway and, across the sea, Fingal's Cave at Staffa off the island of Mull. There are columnar basalts on Rathlin, the most interesting being at the small promontory of Doon Point, on the east coast. Here, curved columns drop into the sea and others radiate in all directions. It is a compact exposure and well worth seeing, as the columns are as precise as any at the Giant's Causeway. Another cluster of radiating columns, known as the 'sun rock', is high on the cliffs north of the West Lighthouse, only visible from a boat. Columns form when fine-grained lavas cool slowly, shrinking and cracking like mud on a pond that has dried out. Unlike the mud cracks, a surface feature, the cooling in the lavas travels through the flow, producing long columns, which tend to fracture horizontally as well, and movements in the lava flow can create curved columns.

Faster cooling, especially when the thickening lavas are inundated with fresh water, results in much more irregular forms. Lava erupting below the sea will produce rounded lumps known as 'pillow lavas'.

On Rathlin, as in much of County Antrim, the spectacular columnar features are the exception – the norm is the covering of lower basalts that make up the huge dark cliffs, in which many layers can be seen, each representing a former lava flow, and the considerable areas of the basalt type that sometimes contains precise columns, known as tholeitic basalt, the scenery of which has already been discussed.

Some of the more prominent features in Rathlin's volcanic landscape were produced by intrusions. These occur when further eruptions force lava through weak points in existing flows, creating long, wall-like extensions known as dykes, and, being more resistant to erosion, these can also appear as mounds, hills and even massive cliffs, as on much of Fair Head. Dolerite is the more coarse-grained basalt that forms many of these features, as mentioned above.

The Rocky Road to Improvement

Economic geology is probably the term for this short account, describing the use islanders have made of the rocks, clays and the water trapped amongst these. Until cement, modern bricks and concrete blocks could be shipped to the island in heavy loads on the modern vehicle ferry, locally quarried basalt and chalk was used for building. An outstanding exception was the construction of the West Lighthouse over the years 1912-1916. Huge amounts of concrete were needed, everything being landed at a pier at Cooraghy, where a long ramp was used to haul loads to the cliff top for transport to the site.

The earliest exploitation of Rathlin's rocks was by Mesolithic and Neolithic peoples around 7,000 to 5,000 years ago. The numerous flints within the chalk were fashioned into tools. At Brockley, outcrops of *porcellanite*, a hard blue-black rock formed by the action of volcanic heat on weathered basalt, were quarried by Neolithic occupants of the island and worked up to create distinctive, highly polished stone axe heads. These were exported to many parts of Britain and Ireland. I've held one of the larger axe heads: it is surprisingly heavy, very smooth and has a sharp cutting edge. Some were so large and perfectly finished it is believed they may have had ritual rather than practical uses. The only other known porcellanite outcrop – also worked to produce axes – was at Tievebulliagh above Cushendall on the Antrim mainland.

Evidence of local sources of stone is found in the many small, abandoned quarries that can be found scattered about the island. Nature is reclaiming these, vegetation slowly greening the sites and birds finding nesting places in crevices and on ledges. It used to be that you could identify the underlying geology at different parts of the island by looking at the roads: those around Church Bay were vivid white with chalk stones and dust, elsewhere they were dark with 'redds' (small quarry stones) of basalt and in places both occurred, giving a pied appearance to tracks. Gradually, however, black tarmac is creeping over the island's roads, signposts have sprouted but thankfully, as yet, no traffic lights have appeared!

There are more stone walls than hedges on Rathlin. These walls are mainly of a dry stone construction, although some may now have thin caps of concrete. The most striking are those made of chalk, and along the coast road from the old pier to Mill Bay there are fine examples, with superb gate pillars showing conical tops. There was a tradition elsewhere in Ulster of topping a few gate pillars with a flatter surface, so that the fairies could dance on them. The steeply coned Rathlin pillars suggest sure-footed fairies. Care needs to be taken not to dislodge stones or collapse these walls by climbing over them.

About half way along the white cliffs in Church Bay is the old pier of Killeany. From about 1914 to around 1928, chalk was quarried here, blasting it from the cliff faces and trundling wagon loads on a rail track out along the pier – longer than now – to waiting steamers. These took the chalk to Glasgow where it went on to steel smelters. A number of islanders were employed in this work, as described by Morrison (2003). Elsewhere, smaller chalk quarries were opened for local use. There are several remains of lime kilns about the island.

Excavations at the ruins of old settlements at Ally in Carravinally townland on the south arm of the island, reported in 2007, showed that red clay was used as a base for paving blocks, and black and white beach stones were inlaid in some floors. There are a few clay beds on the island and numerous beach stones.

Water is another resource that the rock layers yield. The amounts trapped within and between layers in the basalts and chalk may not be large. Most of the island's water supplies now come from boreholes in the basalts on the western arm; formerly the lakes and numerous springs and wells supplied domestic water. With so much chalk underlying the island's dark cap of basalt, one might expect *aquifers* (underground reservoirs of water). However, this chalk is not the porous rock most notable in southern England's white cliffs. It is denser, with the spaces that occur in the English chalk filled with calcite, thus partly inhibiting water flow. Nevertheless, the island's geology does not exclude water; it percolates through cracks in the basalt and lies in pockets where further drainage is impeded by thin layers of almost impervious red volcanic dusts. It also finds its way through some of the chalk. The water often seeps out and such seepages can be spotted on the rocky shores by the presence of bright green seaweeds. The island is well served by springs and wells, providing water sources for generations of islanders. However, these were subject to contamination and vulnerable to drought, and today most of the wells are abandoned and water is supplied from boreholes and reservoirs, regularly tested and with a minimum of chemical purifiers. The water is good but the present supply may not match the growing demand as tourism increases. Some agricultural water supplies are still sourced from lakes and other wetlands.

Exploring Rathlin's Geology

There are now many excellent books that popularise the geology of Ulster; the northern part of Ireland that takes in nine counties. Perhaps all of the above has left you thinking that the island's geology is a bit more complicated than the overall black and white appearance suggests, but in fact it is only as complicated as you make it. My general interest in rocks takes me around certain parts of Rathlin. At the risk of a little repetition, the following summary might encourage you to explore some of the island's geological features.

A boat trip is a good way to see the layers in the cliffs that demonstrate former lava flows, the wonderful narrow caves along the north side where marine and freshwater algae colour these pink and green, while mosses, liverworts and ferns add to the show, and a boat also helps you get closer to the details of the fantastically eroded chalk. Scrambles to the shore at Doon Bay and area reveal amazing columns and nearby there are subtle geological features on the broken foreshore of Maddygalla Dyke; another scramble down the grassy slope at Roonivoolin brings you to a mixed chalk and basalt shore, with huge, black, rolled flints in the chalk; the bay at Cooraghy, along the western side, is another place to see the salt and pepper mix of chalk and basalt and find caves.

The golden rule is to be sensible – do not risk climbing on any of these rocks, be sure you have permission if you leave roads and way-marked tracks and watch those tides! I am not a formally trained geologist, but Rathlin has taught me a lot while trying to understand how the many millions of years have contributed to a story of sea sediments hardened to chalk and of great volcanic outpourings of lava that cooled to make the basalts. Happy hunting!

4. GREEN IS MY VALLEY

Farming on an Island

An aerial view of Rathlin shows scarps and valleys along the rugged western arm, green fields about Church Bay and a mix of ridges and hollows on the south arm. Medium and small lakes glint and all is surrounded by blue sea. The basalt overlay has weathered to give quite good soils and the chalk substrate in an arc around Church Bay also provides fair land. Rough pasture and rocky heath dominate much of the land. It is a green and fertile island.

People have lived on Rathlin for a long time. Prior to the eighteenth century we can only speculate about how the land was used, although recent archaeological work on the island has revealed evidence of grain use in the Bronze Age and no doubt will turn up more information. A timeline for agriculture can be constructed from the 1740s when the Gage family became landlords, leasing most of the island from the Earl of Antrim.

In the second half of the eighteenth century, the island, densely populated, was tilled in small plots where shelter and soils permitted. Barley seems to have been a major crop, along with oats. Potatoes were widely grown, even in 'hanging gardens' on steep slopes and below cliffs where access was possible. Smaller crops of oats, wheat, beans and flax were produced. Sheep and cattle were kept, as well as goats. Horses were widespread, essential working animals, and hay plus a significant part of the grain crops grown were used as feed for them.

Little probably changed within farming for a couple of hundred years except that the population declined, for example from 1010 in 1841 to 753 in 1851, and is currently around 100; the decline is particularly notable following the 1840s potato crop failures known as the Great Famine. Many smallholdings were abandoned. Emigration, however, also took place before this event.

In 1720, the landlord of Rathlin was the Earl of Antrim and on top of the annual rent there was an expectation of duties. These were paid in kind with 144 pullets (young domestic fowl) and 70 sheep. By 1784, when the Reverend Doctor Hamilton visited the island in July, there was a new landlord (Gage) and the rent was £600 that year. Rathlin's population then was around 1200 people. Hamilton's comments on agriculture are sparse, but he mentioned barley as a significant crop with, in a good year, £600 worth being exported to Scotland, usually for whisky (*whisky* in Scotland, *whiskey* in Ireland) production. He noted good sheep produced on 'craggy pastures' and praised the island's horses as sure-footed, making use of one to explore Rathlin.

Dr. Marshall, visiting in 1834, is more detailed, as befits the observant eye of a medical doctor. He described crops of barley, oats, wheat, flax, potatoes and also mentioned barley exports, specifying Scotland, quoting an annual export of 90 tons. Describing the islanders' foods, he listed potatoes, oaten and barley breads, fish and their home produced mutton, pork and occasionally beef, although cattle were mainly exported to Ballycastle, as were potatoes. Thus there were cattle, sheep and pigs reared, and goats are also listed. In 1861, as described by McCurdy (2000), 75 tenancies (involving about 450 people) took in

Green Is My Valley

1082 hectares (2676 acres), a considerable proportion of the island. Both Hamilton and Marshall mention kelp production from seaweeds, discussed in the later chapter about the shores and coastal waters.

Photographs of the area around Church Bay about 1915 show neatly walled fields with a predominance of cultivated land and very little ground cover. Morrison (2003), describing his early days on Rathlin in the 1920s and 1930s, gives a good summary of the yearly cycle of ploughing, planting, tilling and harvesting, with crops of barley, oats and potatoes. When the harvest was safely gathered, attention turned to fishing. McCurdy (2010) describes his childhood on his home farm on the island in the 1930s, showing the interdependence with neighbours and the mix of crops and garden produce essential to the then self-sufficient way of life.

By 1943 the first tractor arrived on the island and agricultural improvement throughout Ulster in the 1950s and 1960s gradually extended to Rathlin, adapted to suit the island's conditions. Hay gave way to silage, tillage died out. From the 1940s to the 1960s, a key farmer on the island was 'King' Tony McCuaig. His honorary title reflected his role as a community leader. During our bird observatory days on Rathlin in 1960 and 1961, we would often gather in Tony's pub (now a private house) at Demesne above Church Bay, only to be ejected sooner than we expected as he was an early-to-bed and early-to-rise busy farmer as well as publican. At this time he ran a substantial beef cattle herd, kept 300 ewes and had ten acres (4 hectares) in potatoes and oats.

In the 1980s and 1990s some progressive farming altered parts of the landscape on the western arm, with conversion of heath and rough grazing to more intensive grasslands. These very green swathes are still visible but are now gradually becoming part of a more environmentally sympathetic way of farming, including organic production.

Greer (1994) lists the numbers of cattle on Rathlin from 1981 to 1992, the figures ranging from 414 to 634 in any one year, and reports that, in 1991, there were 438 cattle and about 1200 sheep on the island. Today cattle and sheep are the mainstay of agriculture here, supported by pasturage and silage crops. Vegetables are still grown, mostly in gardens and at the Manor House (organic), as well as on one of the organic farms within poly-tunnel units. There are three farmers involved with organic production of cattle for beef, as well as sheep. The agricultural landscape of Rathlin is less obvious than on the mainland, where farmland extends to the edge of the cliffs, neat fields with trimmed hedges dominate the lower ground and the uplands are a mix of sheep pasture, rough grazing, blanket bog, heathland and extensive blocks of commercial forestry. Rathlin's improved grasslands, organic grazing areas and its bits of forest (see below) are part of an uneven landscape of hills and valleys, rocky outcrops, moorland and lakes.

You can walk the accessible routes and not realise that there's quite a number of farm animals. On a fine summer's day, cattle might be spotted on the cliff tops, but mostly they are grazing in fields tucked into the contours, while sheep can be encountered roving about the rougher grazing lands. Here and there you might find a cluster of horses and around some of the farms and dwellings the clucking of hens or the quack of ducks might be heard. The glint of silage bales wrapped in black plastic remind us that farming here is as modern as on the mainland, if on a smaller scale. It is, however, worth remembering the added challenges and costs for an island farmer: the transport of animals to and from the mainland, the need to ship in fuel, feed, machinery and everything else required to run a farm and the hire of contractors for certain jobs. The weather can disrupt the best laid plans, perhaps resulting in a missed market or a vet delayed.

Farming and Wildlife

The effects of agriculture on wildlife are perhaps less than on the mainland. The change from grain crops to grass must have reduced feeding for small birds, as the corn bunting and yellowhammer, two noted seed-eaters, were described as common on the island in the nineteenth century, as were twite, linnet and house sparrow. Interestingly, both greenfinch and goldfinch, now resident and breeding, were then described as mainly winter visitors while lesser redpoll was scarce. Today, seed eating birds depend mainly on the wild flora and agricultural grasslands, and the autumn and winter are the best time to see flocks of linnet, twite, snow bunting and others. The corncrake eventually vanished, hanging on as a breeding bird longer than anywhere else in Northern Ireland. The increase in grazed pasture benefited others, such as chough and other crows but the former is now rare. Hooded crows and ravens have carrion to feed on at lambing time and a dead rabbit or hare is soon spotted. The forest has attracted birds that might never have been common on Rathlin, such as tits, lesser redpolls and long-eared owls. Ferrets were brought to Rathlin in 1988 to assist in rabbit control and are now well established and a predator of ground nesting birds. A game-shooting project in the 1990s also had its effects, with feed-crops grown and a gamekeeper present. The island still has a few red-legged partridges and pheasants wandering about, hungry for hand-outs that no longer appear.

A number of environmental projects operate on the island through the Department of Agriculture and Rural Development's programme known as the Countryside Management Scheme and the older Environmentally Sensitive Areas designation. At present (2010), there are nine Rathlin landowners involved in what is known as agri-environment schemes, taking in 526 hectares, which is around 36% of the island's area. These projects are focused mainly on semi-natural grassland and dry heath, two valuable habitats on Rathlin, with other work on grasslands, scrub, breeding bird (waders) sites and more. There is also a stone wall restoration project, more of which is needed.

The Fragmented Forest

Rathlin today has few trees. Those that manage to survive the salt winds and winter storms cling to sheltered parts of the island's varied terrain, usually providing some shelter to dwellings, occupied or in ruin. There is a small wind-pruned deciduous plantation from the Manor House to Church Brae, containing mostly sycamore, some alder and a few other species.

Remains of ancient trees have been found in Rathlin bogs. The island was populated, probably thinly, from at least the start of the

Neolithic period and the local production of high grade stone axes most probably helped these early settlers to clear what woodland existed on good soil for farming. Agriculture continued in the Bronze Age but later in that period the climate became cooler and wetter and acid peat bogs began to spread, no doubt making life difficult for the remaining trees (and farmers).

Thus the island was probably almost tree-less for a long time. State-supported conifer forestry arrived when an experimental planting on 60 hectare (150 acres) at the western end of the island, commenced in 1955-56 and spread over humps and hollows of former rocky heath and grassland. A few islanders were employed to prepare the ground by digging drainage ditches and to plant the young trees. One resident's account of this work mentions spruce, pine, larch, willow, hazel and oak, but he comments that only the pine, spruce and willow survived. Rabbits feasted on the young tree shoots until suitable fencing was erected, then later in the 1950s myxomatosis thinned the rabbit population but the fencing still required maintenance.

Today, the 'forest' remains spread in patches of medium-tall spruce and pine in sheltered hollows, plus a few larch groves. You can find distorted and wind-pruned trees clinging to slopes and other exposed sites, individuals that would grace any Japanese-designed garden. From certain parts of the island, the jagged tops of the taller trees can be seen undulating across the skyline like over-sized dark green caterpillars, but most of this unexpected habitat is tucked away out of sight, trees keeping their heads down and trying to survive the wild weather that the Atlantic Ocean often flings at Rathlin.

This fragmented forest could be said to be a failure as none of the timber is worth harvesting, but it has done its bit to increase island biodiversity, attracting woodland birds, moths and other insects. It was neither extensive in cover nor geometrically laid out and thus never dominated the landscape in the way some big commercial plantations have across the water in mainland County Antrim.

5. ISLAND FLOWER GARDEN

Seasons of Colour

At first glance, Rathlin's rugged features and its position in a turbulent sea, swept by salty winds, may give the impression that it's a daunting place for wild flowers and other plants to thrive, trees included. However, if you arrive between April to September, you will find the island vibrant with flowers. A floral list published in 1994 and up-dated to 2008 records almost 500 species of native and introduced plants. There are plenty of places (habitats) for plants to get hold and flourish. As far as various census data tells us, Rathlin had a human population of between 1000 and 1200 from 1784 to 1841 and the agriculture necessary to feed such a density of people and their stock would have produced a much-tilled landscape. The need for fuel led to removal of most of the island's workable peat and probably whatever trees were available. Today there are fewer people living on Rathlin (around 100) and farming is reliant on beef cattle and sheep and consequently there is emphasis on pasture and silage production. Nevertheless, the worst excesses of intensive farming seemed to have been avoided and there are many features that help to sustain a varied flora. What are generally called 'wetlands' – lakes, ponds, marshes, bogs, fens and suchlike - are given a chapter of their own immediately after this one, where their flora is discussed along with animal life and other features.

A seasonal approach may be the best way to describe the island's botanical richness. All that I've described below can be seen by following the network of island roads and permitted off-road tracks as well as exploring the more accessible parts of the shores. There are plants listed in the 2008 flora that I have not yet found, so there are ample opportunities for surprises and perhaps some new finds if you are interested in botany.

Spring

Come in April in the time of *primroses* and *violets* and the first *early purple orchids*. The moorland is still clad in winter browns and reed-beds are a warm buff with glinting blue water between them.

The *gorse* along the drier hills and escarpments is lit up with vivid yellow flowers giving out a scent of coconut as you brush past these prickly bushes. In gardens *daffodils* wave at you and the road verges and field banks, most so far un-sprayed with herbicides and infrequently cut, are full of early wildflowers such as *celandine*, *dandelion*, *primrose*, vivid white *stitchwort*, violets and the little white stars of *wild strawberry*. Why are so many spring flowers yellow and white? Such flowers are generalists in terms of attracting pollinators and these colours attract the first bumble bees, hoverflies and a few butterflies. Other colours and more complex flower structures are evident as spring passes into summer.

In the patch of woodland beyond the harbour, near the Manor House, the ground is carpeted in April with the long-stemmed white flowers of *three-cornered leek,* an introduced species often found near large houses. They are not to be confused with the smaller but related wild garlic or *ramsons*, more widespread in mainland woods in spring.

Here and there amongst the brown heaths and heather vegetation are splashes of pale green leaves of *Montbretia*, a garden escape well established in Ireland. Its vivid orange flowers come later in summer. It can be fun to try and spot plants before they flower – some are easier to identify than others which might leave you with damp knees after a close look. Always take the book to the flower and resist picking it.

Rathlin's rocky coast, short maritime grasslands and pebble and cobble beaches are a delight for flower finders. May is the peak month for colour and vigour with white, pink, pale blue, deep and pale yellows and the occasional flash of red, nature's palette being generous at this time. *Scurvy grass* (not a grass but related to cabbage) is white and sweetly scented and can be found all around the shores in April and May and even later. There are two species and the leaves are rich in vitamin C and were indeed once collected by sailors as a preventative treatment against the vitamin C deficiency condition known as scurvy. The leaves are very bitter – I've tried them and prefer to suck an orange for my vitamin C. Then there are *sea pinks* galore, varying from pale to almost red, sprouting from the cushions of narrow green leaves; deep yellow *bird's-foot trefoil*, often with a touch of red on the petals, giving them another common name 'eggs and bacon'; pale blue *spring squill* can be found on short cliff-top grasslands, light yellow *kidney vetch* clusters on the cliff slopes, notably on chalk, and white *sea campion*, greenish-yellow *sea plantain* and so on, lots of variety, masses of colour – you'd be hard pressed to create such perfect rockeries.

Rathlin has many old walls and they are worth a search, looking out in spring for the little blue and yellow flowers of *ivy-leaved toadflax*, the fleshy red leaves of *English stonecrop* (flowers later) and the green fronds of small ferns such as *rusty-back* and *maidenhair spleenwort*.

Spring on Rathlin rewards the diligent searcher, but you can also enjoy much by just wandering the roads, lanes and seashore and keeping alert for flashes of colour and green promises of things to come. In terms of flowering, if Rathlin is waking up in April, it has leapt out of bed in May.

Summer

In these cool climes on Northern Ireland's most northerly piece of land it can be tricky to be sure when it is spring or if summer has arrived. Some experts turn to maps of seasonal isotherms, which are lines joining areas of equal temperature. The spring isotherm for this part of the world is 10 degrees C and the line of it sweeps close to Rathlin with the date tags 9 February to 21 March, suggesting a start to spring at this latitude. Another chart, showing the northward advance of arriving swallows shows 15 April to 1 May as the date brackets when we might expect to see these birds arrive, moving north through the UK and Ireland (Newton, 2010). On Rathlin, one swallow might hint at spring but it takes many more to define summer.

So, on the island I stick my neck out and suggest late March through to the end of May as 'spring' and June through to the end of August as 'summer' as far as flower seasons are concerned (and probably also insects, birds and mammals). Island farmers have their own measures for the seasons and their interests in spring lie in the much welcomed first flush of new grasses and the ground drying out enough to enable machinery to be taken into the fields.

What's flowering in June? Lots, really, as many spring flowers continue to bloom and are joined by others. Insects become much more active, and have a wide choice for nectar and pollen. It's a great month for orchids – early purples are still flowering, and the rough grassland and heaths are full of *spotted orchids* and their hybrids, small, pinkish-purple and often but not always with spotted leaves. Around the shores, sea pinks continue to flower, gradually going to seed as the petals become like crisp brown paper, and are joined by *yellow silverweed,* a creeping plant with silver undersides to its leaves. Tall *tree mallows* with pink flowers grow close to the harbour towards St Thomas's church and turn up in other places, including out on one of the precipitous sea stacks in the far west. Along walls and hedges red and purple *fuchsia* is a-hum with bees. *Honeysuckle* is widespread and is another plant loud with bees and hoverflies. On walls look out for small little tightly clustered yellow flower-heads of *medick* and pinkish white flowers of *English stonecrop* and its yellow and peppery-tasting relative, *biting stonecrop.* On basalt cliffs and on some walls are the sky-blue, tightly-flowered heads of *sheep's bit (*scabious family).

A good tip is to carry a pair of binoculars, very useful for spotting plants at a distance in areas where you would not wish to trespass or on cliff faces out of reach but well worth scanning from a safe vantage point.

July is summer whatever the weather. *Valerian* leans out in clusters from walls, and it can be red, pink or white. *Honeysuckle* continues to spread its sweet scent from gardens and hedges and walls, and in the lakes yellow *water lilies* are plentiful. The vivid purple *bell heather* is beginning to flower on dry and rocky ground. Cleg-followed and cleg-bitten (clegs are one of a family of biting flies), I have cycled and walked Rathlin's byeways in July to enjoy creamy *hogweed* full of orange soldier beetles, blue *harebells* with flowers porcelain thin, fragrant ivory coloured *meadowsweet,* purple *thistles* covered with butterflies and more, almost falling off the bike as my gaze is captured by flowers and insects. On the moors, yellow *bog asphodel* is everywhere and little gold crosses of *tormentil* wink at you.

August is good for purple: *devil's bit scabious* (short roots where the Devil has crept along underground and bitten them off) and clumps of *wild thyme* carpeting rocks and walls. Rathlin puts on one of its best floral displays this month, when the purple bell heather and the mustard yellow *western gorse* flower together on the dry heaths. This is a different species of gorse to the spring plant, a shrub never taller than its purple heathy companion, and the two form dense cover on many parts of the island, at their best on the heathland near the East Lighthouse, part of a designated Area of Special Scientific Interest (see Appendices for explanation of such designations). Yellow again, in *ragwort, hawkweed* (a tricky group to separate the species), and tall and soft-spiked *sow thistle.* By now all the grasses are going from flower to seed, with twittering goldfinches and other seed-eaters in attendance.

Autumn

By September, the lilac to pale purple of *ling* (common heather) takes over from the vivid display described of summer and Rathlin's heathery moorlands buzz with bees. There are a number of bee-keepers on the island, so not all these bees are bumbles – you will see honeybees as well as hoverflies.

There is still quite a lot of colour about, many of the August species flowering into September and even October, but autumn is seed time, laying down the guarantees for next year, and by October colours change to tawny and reddish on the moors and in the wet areas, an indicator of the changing season. This seems a brief statement for a lovely time of year, but it's a time when birds are on the move, when my binoculars rise from peering at plants to look to the skies.

Winter

Floristically, the island has drifted off to sleep. That's not to say you can't be surprised by a sea pink in flower in some sheltered nook in the cliffs or a few summer flowers that haven't been watching their calendar. It's also a time, if you are a real botanist with a bent back and a grasp of Latin, to be able to spot small plants by their winter foliage, amongst dormant vegetation which in spring and summer would hide these gems.

Umbrellas in Summer

There is a family of flowers – the carrot family – with the Latin tag *Umbelliferae*. The entire flower heads of members of this group looks like an opened umbrella, sometimes flat-topped like a Japanese parasol but there are many curved true umbrella-like examples. The whiter varieties, seen from a distance, can look like mushrooms. The arrangement of the florets, grouped on stalks like the spokes of an umbrella, complete the likeness to our familiar rain-repelling companion.

These umbrella flowers - the flower arrangements are known as *umbels* – vary in colour from white and creamy-white to pinkish-mauve and yellow or greenish yellow. Some are sweet-smelling, others musky, a number are edible and a few are poisonous and one is dangerous in another way, its stems armed with bristles that can raise nasty blisters on contact with naked skin. All are interesting, eye-catching and Rathlin has its fair share of them, about 18 species listed so far. The various types flower from March to November and some can be found in bloom throughout the year. Nevertheless, many are summer umbrellas, and what follows is a selection of the more visible and commoner ones (and one scarcer alien) that brighten Rathlin's landscapes.

An obvious starter is the *wild carrot*, shin to knee height and common on Rathlin and flowering mostly in June and July. Favouring chalky and other dry soils, it is at home near the coast as well as road and field verges and in rough grasslands. As the flower heads open, they are flattish and are pink to reddish. They soon curve into shallow white umbrellas, often with a wine-splash of reddish-purple in the centre. As they go to seed, the flower-heads become green and shrink to concave somewhat untidy clusters, often known as 'birds'-nests'. The feathery carrot-like leaves and pale roots smell of carrot, but the latter is skinny and never swells to the familiar and orange carrot we know so well. The domestic vegetable cultivated so widely originated in a Mediterranean variety of this plant. The wild carrot is one of the most attractive of the high-summer umbellifers and its flowers, like those of most of its relatives, are frequently dotted with flies and other small insects.

A larger and more robust umbrella flower, and probably the commonest and most widespread on the island, is *hogweed*, flowering from June to September, although you can find some in bloom throughout the year. As the name suggests, it has a pig connection, used mainly in Britain in the past as pig fodder. Pigs clearly have good taste, for the younger shoots and leaves are said to have a similar flavour to asparagus. The stout hollow stems were – when kids had less toys – popular for making pea-shooters (beware! see the next species). Hogweed is normally knee to thigh high but can, in shady areas and under woodland cover in competition for the light, shoot up to an adult's eye level. The flower-heads are not as curved and umbrella-like as some other members of the family, and are generally creamy rather than pure white. The leaves are quite broad and the plant can sometimes be hairy. It is not hard to spot on Rathlin, even occurring on cliffs and steep slopes.

Although hogweed can be robust and tall, it never measures up, both in size and reputation, to its foreign and invasive namesake the *giant hogweed*, flowering mainly in June. This plant, although listed in the Rathlin flora, is scarce here, but you would know it at once on sight, or at least say "what on Earth is that?" The pale green stem cylinders are covered in purple blotches and stiff bristly hairs like small hypodermics. It can grow to over 3 metres (almost ten feet) and produces a wide canopy made up of cartwheels of creamy umbels. Everything about this strangely beautiful plant shouts 'alien!'

The stem spines, penetrating or just brushing your skin, give rise to a polysyllabic condition I won't attempt to spell that manifests in raised blisters and larger areas of skin that appear burned, which in fact they more or less are, for the plant's sap reduces the skin's ability to cope with sunlight. Sometimes children cut the dried stems after the flowering season to make blow-pipes or pea-shooters, often with quite serious results. This plant is a native of Asia and has been an exotic garden favourite in Britain and Ireland for about 150 years. At some stage, generally believed to be around the 1970s, it got over the estate walls and spread into our nice safe countryside. Usually it is found by streams and rivers or along roadsides, for its seeds float and are light enough to be wind-carried in vehicle slipstreams. It also occurs on 'waste' ground. An island friend discovered one huge specimen and, with help, dismantled it in sections and stored these in a sealed plastic barrel in a shed, where it rotted to an evil smelling brown sludge. It is striking and rather beautiful in full flower, but admire it from a distance. In our extremely health and safety conscious time, this plant's presence near human habitation is enough for local officials to wage war on it. In the press, reports use language decorated with terms such as 'dangerous alien', 'triffids' and so on, and teams of plant-assassins try cutting, digging-out, massive doses of chemicals and even fire, yet often still fail to eradicate it.

While on the hogweed/ pig theme, the much smaller ankle-high umbrella of short grassy places is *pignut,* typically a flower of May and often found in Ireland alongside bluebells that brave the light away from woods (or have had the woods removed from above them). It is a familiar sight in short turf and in some dry heaths on Rathlin. The name comes from the habit of foraging pigs rooting for it with enthusiasm.

From pigs to cows: the delicate white flower-heads of *cow parsley,* often known in Ireland as 'Lady's Lace' and placed on altars in chapels to decorate the Virgin Mary's place of honour, is a familiar sight along road verges in May and June. It is quite widespread on Rathlin, not just by roads but also along hedge and wall banks and in uncut meadows. It is the best known umbellifer, and on rural roads where early cutting or spraying by the tidy brigade has not occurred, a nostalgic reminder of what all our road verges were like before today's obsession with tidiness. It is not an actively gathered cow-fodder plant, and the name is possibly linked to a perception of a poor quality parsley type not fit for anything except to be browsed by freedom-seeking cattle munching their way through the 'long acre' of countryside road verges.

To my mind, the most attractive of the summer umbrellas is the delightfully named and later flowering (July to September) *wild angelica* (I like the idea of wild angels). Sprouting large, densely packed almost cauliflower-like cream blooms, these are reminiscent of luscious green-stalked mushrooms from a distance. You'll find them along Rathlin's wild road verges, in her meadows, rough grasslands and grassy slopes overlooking the sea. Once fully formed, the flower-heads are truly umbrella-like and are usually covered with small flies, hoverflies and other little insects that fall prey to the orange soldier beetles that patrol the flowers. The leaves are distinctively sharp-toothed. This plant's relative the *garden angelica* is the one whose candied stems we use for decorating cakes (those of us who still bake and decorate cakes).

Wild angelica is normally knee to thigh high but can, like many of its equally robust cousins, reach chest high if forced to compete for light.

Sometimes what is not there is just as interesting and one umbellifer that is widespread along the north coast and is scarce on Rathlin (I haven't found it yet but it is listed) is *alexanders,* a thigh to waist high parsley-like plant with yellowish-green flower heads that flourish from March to at least June. It should deserve a capital letter as it was known as 'the parsley of Alexandria', a herb known to the Egyptians and the Greeks and valued for many medicinal uses. The shiny green leaves are noticeable as early as February along coastal road verges. It produces enormous quantities of seeds and has spread along traffic corridors, aided by vehicle and train slipstreams.

One more umbrella, this time not of the umbelliferous family but a lookalike from the daisy clan, is the feathery-leaved *yarrow,* with a long flowering season from June to November. The little yarrow canopies are flattish to gently curved and can be cream or pinkish-mauve. Rarely much higher than your walking boot, it is widespread on Rathlin and can be spotted almost anywhere, from verges to grasslands to occasionally poking a head above the shorter dry heaths. It's a pleasure to find, especially in autumn when there are fewer flowers. Yarrow has a long folk history and is discussed in the folklore section, but it's worth saying here that it is a love charm, frequently picked and taken home for secret and hopeful rituals by girls seeking luck in romance. It thrives on Rathlin and throughout Ireland – maybe computer dating has taken over from collecting flower charms!

Vagabonds and Gatecrashers

What exactly is a weed? Definitions tend to be general rather than exact: the New Penguin Dictionary (2000) says a weed is a wild plant that grows where it is not wanted and spreads over or chokes out cultivated plants. In a biological sense, there's no such thing as a weed; it is a cultural definition, a human invention, a plant in the wrong place. Richard Mabey, in his cultural history of weeds (2010), asks what is the right place? There are places where we want no plants at all, for example pavements, roads, many buildings. The word seems to have entered the English language in its current form around 1200 as *wede*, from Old English *weod*, grass or herb. It had equivalents in Old Saxon, Middle Dutch and Old High German and prior to 800 the Old English word *uueodhoc* meant a 'weedhook', a tool for cutting weeds. No doubt the first Neolithic farmers knew what they were dealing with as unwanted plants invaded their crops and they, like many of us today, suffered the back-breaking task of rooting them out.

Growing and spreading of weeds is defined, in the language of war and violence, as invading, penetrating, dominating, strangling etc. Weeds are treated as insurgents, to be defeated at any cost. Gardeners, local authorities, builders and others yank them up, dig them out, cut them down, spray them with poisons, burn them – the list of assaults is long. They are even buried alive under concrete and tarmac, some being able to punch their way through to the air and the light.

Weeds seem to be tolerated on Rathlin, even in most of the agricultural landscape, and thus add greatly to the plant diversity of the island, or, as I prefer to view this, providing colour, vigour and the occasional surprise. Whether it is in fact tolerance or just less of the tidy-minded applications of gardeners and local authorities and road managers is hard to say. A bit of both, I would guess. Rathlin's road verges, banks and field edges receive less attention from the cutters and pruners and sprayers, although in June (2010) I noted, with trepidation, a van and trailer carrying spraying equipment and jars full of liquid labelled 'dangerous for the environment' on the ferry over to the island. However, this contractor seemed to be working only along the harbour, the waterfront and 'main roads' close to Church Bay. But the weeds will have their way – clearance of long-standing verge plants just offers the more aggressive and eventually herbicide resistant varieties to establish. Rather than a diverse range of wild flowers decorating these verges and banks, chemical treatment will likely produce an impoverished habitat rampant with a few species of more persistent 'weeds'.

Mabey examines our long (almost 10,000 years) association with those plants which have been our constant companions since we first started to disturb soils. Plants we consider as weeds have survival strategies that make them very successful: some have rapid life cycles, such as the *groundsel* which can go from seed to flower and seed again in six weeks; or individual plants can produce huge numbers of seeds, one survey of alexanders for example demonstrated that 75,000 plants produced 450 million seeds weighing 22 metric tonnes. Seeds themselves can demonstrate tremendous periods of dormancy, 2,000 years in the case of some uncovered at a Roman excavation site.

Many weeds of pastures contain higher levels of minerals essential to ruminant animals than the sown grasses. Plantains and buttercups are rich in cobalt, dandelions and stinging nettles have good concentrations of copper and iron, magnesium is found in ribwort plantain and yarrow, and the bird's foot trefoil can fix nitrogen in the soil as can clovers. Tolerance of a reasonable level of grassland weeds could save farmers on purchases of mineral licks.

Most of us recognise a dandelion, and know that it's almost impossible to pull a well established one up with the root intact. So we reach for the spray. However, throughout the growing season, there are many dandelion-like flowers to confuse the non-botanist, and Rathlin offers a good range of these – *hawkweeds, hawkbits, hawksbeards, cats-ears, ox-tongues* and so on. Intriguing names, yellow flowers mostly and hawk-whatever because hawks have good eyesight and these are supposed to be eyesight-enhancing plants, especially for hawks. I've never seen a hawk eat one, but the name is widespread.

Even the common bindweed is variable. The white variety is plentiful on Rathlin, but there is an attractive roseate variant of the large white one to be found in several places, notably up the stream side of Church Brae. A weed-named species found commonly along shores and in short grasslands is the silverweed (mentioned briefly above), a low almost flattened plant with feathery green leaves that are silvery below. The flower is not unlike a buttercup, but of a paler and not so glossy yellow. It is a most determined spreader, so if it gets into your lawn or stoned areas you might call it a pernicious weed, but it is pretty.

Weeds are great hitch-hikers, whether as seeds on our boots or stuck in the treads of our vehicle tyres, or hooked seeds clinging to our clothes, and light seeds can follow along in the slipstreams of lorries and trains. With two ferries bringing lots of walkers and some vehicles and most of the islanders' goods, there are opportunities for new arrivals of plants. The island roads have been up-graded and have more traffic than in the past. Livestock are imported (and exported) by ferry and the island's soils are now disturbed by construction projects rather than arable agriculture. Opportunistic plants are being presented with lots of chances for rapid colonisation and spread, so Rathlin's flora may be in for a period of change, to which climatic warming could be a significant influence.

However, such is the long-established marginal flora of Rathlin that nowhere on the shores, fields, walls, road verges and elsewhere do I get the feeling that I am looking at weeds: they are all flowers, adding to the glory of colours through the seasons. I hope the tidy-minded brigade is kept under control on the island – weeds have rights, too.

1.1 Rue Point Lighthouse - Photo by Tom McDonnell

1.2 Former coastguard house at Ushet Port

1.3 Rathlin Grey Seals - Photo by Tom McDonnell

1.4 'The Drowned Magpie' - black basalt on white chalk

1.5 Summer heath of bell heather and western gorse

1.6 Rathlin harbour and 18th Century Manor House

1.7 Long-Eared Owls - Photo by Tom McDonnell

1.8 Peregrine Falcon on Rathlin- Photo by Tom McDonnell

1.9 The delicate Harebell

1.10 Male 'Common Darter' Dragonfly – Photo by Alan Watson

1.11 Lobster fishing off West Lighthouse, summer 1999

1.12 Ploughing in the 1930s - Photo courtesy of Loughie McQuaig

1.13 Old agricultural machinery

1.14 A kelp forest at low water, Roonivoolin shore

1.15 Lifting a barrel pot 1972

6. WETLANDS

Rathlin is no desert island. From the air or a high spot the watery and wet places glint like jewels scattered from a broken necklace. Some are open lakes, such as Kebble, Nanskan and Ushet, with relatively little emergent vegetation, others are smaller and with reeds and water lilies encroaching, such as Craigmacaggan, Kinkeel and the two Ally loughs, and there are former loughs and pools that are now filled with reeds and bulrushes and other tall vegetation. Many wet areas are small bog pools, water-filled rock hollows and spring-fed flushes. When you are on foot these watery sites appear and disappear as you crest hills and ridges and descend into hollows and valleys throughout Rathlin's contour-ridden landscape. If your attention is elsewhere, sometimes the first inkling of wetland is a damp feeling seeping over your footwear, for it is very easy to go from dry heath and grassland to something moister.

A smattering of botanical knowledge helps you to recognise where it might be wet underfoot. Heather and bell heather (a heath) like dry ground, but as soon as you begin to find the pale pink flowers of cross-leaved heath, you are in wetter territory. Emerald, gold and ruby sphagnum mosses are the gems of the really wet places, worth keeping clear of both for the sake of your feet and for the fragility of these boggy areas.

Lakes, ponds, bogs and bog pools, rock basin pools, flushes, seepages, fens, marshes, damp grasslands, wet heaths – there's a wide range of watery habitats and hence plenty of wetland plants and wildlife. The lakes support breeding birds such as mallard, teal, tufted duck, feral greylag geese, coot, moorhen, dabchick and water rail. Reedy areas have reed bunting, sedge warbler, grasshopper warbler and herons which wander where they choose. Open water and emerging insects attract swallows, house and sand martins to hawk for food, swooping and dipping like terns. Gulls settle on and by the lakes, a few to breed, many to bathe and preen. Glittering dragonflies and damselflies dart about in season, and there are even some frogs, not a lot and once absent from the island (perhaps escapees or releases from school biology lessons featuring imported tadpoles, who knows?). Bogbean, pink swathes of ragged robin and other wetland plants are to be found in abundance. In winter, other wildfowl arrive in small numbers, notably goldeneye, pochard and occasional parties of geese, such as Greenland white-fronted, brent and barnacle, and whooper swans drop in on their way south from breeding grounds on Iceland, and a few may stay for a while.

Water power has never been a significant resource on the island. There are no rivers and only a few short streams and small burns find their way from higher ground to the sea. Nevertheless, water from Craigmaccagan Lough was channelled via a mill race to drive a corn mill in Mill Bay. The remains of the building stand today, with rusting bits of machinery lying about.

Due to less intensive agriculture on the island there is a lower level of fertiliser run-off and many of the lakes are what is termed *mesotrophic*, that is, they are clear, and with a well balanced flora and fauna not over-enriched by nitrogen and phosphates. Trout occur in Nanskan and Ushet, and freshwater eels are found in several of the loughs. Nanskan means 'lough of the eels'.

One type of wetland that lies close to the sea is a salt marsh, a place where salt-tolerant plants have their roots dipped in brackish water and their leaves, stems and flowers splashed with spray. The largest salt marshes are often in estuarine or other low-lying coastal locations, but on Rathlin, as along the nearby Causeway Coast, small patches of salt marsh can be found on the rocky shores, a little way above the highest tide mark. Flowers to look out for are the sea pink, scurvy grass and marsh arrow grass in spring and early summer, and the lovely daisy-like mauve and yellow sea aster in late summer into early autumn. Various small to medium sized rushes also occur in these habitats, which sometimes can be spotted as a rather bright green strip on the upper shore. Butterflies and moths will venture to these spots, and you can find shore birds such as the long-legged redshank and the pied oystercatcher poking about after insects and small crustaceans.

Dragons and Damsels

These are the jewels of the wetlands. Dragonflies and damselflies are, like the butterflies and moths, colourful, dashing, tricky at times to identify and some are rare. Birders, nature reserve wardens, amateur naturalists, anglers – many are the people who are attracted by these darting aerial daredevils. In the past, they were feared and their elongated shape, darting movements and – close up – spooky bulbous-eyed appearance gave them the name of 'devil's darning needles'. Indeed, there are over 80 folk-names for dragonflies (and damselflies). 'Dragon' perhaps because of the narrow body and outstretched wings – a typical dragon profile. The more elegant and less threatening damselflies are well named. Dragonflies were once thought to bite or sting. Should you experience the rare event of one landing on your arm or hand, it may curve its body as if to sting, and you might notice the chewing motion of the mouthparts as if preparing to bite. It will do neither. See those amazing multi-faceted (compound) eyes and wonder what its image of you might be.

Now we love them and like to watch their amazing flights and hear the papery rustle of wings and see these shimmering appendages catch the sunlight. Their general names are accurate – hawkers hawk, darters dart, chasers chase and skimmers skim. Few can watch a dragonfly dart and hover and not think of a helicopter in miniature, but no helicopter or its pilot could match the flying skill of these dragons and damsels of the wetlands.

Underwater, the larval stages of dragonflies are creeping, snatching killers, with powerful jaws capable of chomping even a tadpole.

Eventually they attach themselves to the stems of water plants, pupate and one day in spring an amazing metamorphosis takes place and in time the new dragonfly struggles free from its case, pumps fluids into the wings to expand them and, warming in the sun, takes off on its maiden flight, something few of us see, except on a TV nature programme.

Rathlin, well endowed with watery places, hosts at least 9 species. These are the common spreadwing, azure bluet, common bluet, common bluestrip, spring redtail, moorland hawker, four-spotted chaser, black darter and common darter. Not as imaginative names as the moths but certainly descriptive. Look out for them in summer at lakes, bog pools and damp places in general.

7. BUTTERFLIES and MOTHS

The butterflies and larger moths of Rathlin were little known until the Rankin brothers, two keen young naturalists who spent long holidays at Portballintrae on the north Antrim coast, studied them (along with birds) in the 1930s up to the outbreak of World War Two. Little new was added to their work on Rathlin until the 1980s when RSPB wardens residing on the island for periods began to trap and record moths and observe butterflies. This, along with work by visiting moth enthusiasts, has brought the list of larger moths on Rathlin to over 200 species. There are at least 16 species of butterfly recorded for the island as of 2010.

Perhaps it's not surprising to find birdwatchers and professional ornithologists taking an interest in moths and butterflies. Like the birds, there is a great variety of species, many are colourful, quite a lot are migratory, some provide considerable identification challenges and a number are rare. All these are attributes attractive to the birder, and wardens need to be good all-round naturalists. The work of such enthusiasts in the past two decades has shown Rathlin to be an important site for such insects.

The Admirals and the Painted Lady

On a warm August day, walking up the bare and stony track past clumps of purple heath and yellow western gorse towards the Watch Hut at Cantruan, a medium sized greyish butterfly flits ahead of me, alighting on the bare ground from time to time and closing its wings. Its camouflage is so good – grey and brown against the weathered basalt stones of the track – that it is almost invisible until it flies again. It is a grayling, a tricky butterfly to see due to its inconspicuous colouring. It favours well-drained sunny sites like this path in Ballyconagan Townland near the East Lighthouse and is also found elsewhere on Rathlin, notably at Kebble National Nature Reserve.

Apart from the more locally distributed dark green fritillary, the butterflies of Rathlin are all fairly widespread throughout Northern Ireland. A total of at least 16 species is quite good for an offshore island, and is due mainly to the variety of habitats and relative lack of agricultural intensification on the island, factors also influencing the diversity of moths and many other creatures.

Although many of the butterflies are resident, breed on the island and hibernate over winter, some are also migrants which can arrive in considerable numbers from spring through to autumn. The abundance of flowering thistles on Rathlin in late summer and early autumn attracts red admiral and painted lady butterflies to feed on the energy-giving nectar, where they are often joined by small tortoiseshells, making a colourful spectacle on the flower-heads.

In May the spectacular peacock butterfly may be seen flying from flower to flower, perhaps a bit ragged-winged after winter hibernation. Later, perfect newly emerged adults can be enjoyed and this is a butterfly that can be spotted over many months of the year.

Butterflies lay their eggs on selected plants that will provide food for their caterpillars. Knowing which food plant is favoured by particular species helps you to search for butterflies.

On Rathlin, seek out the bright yellow bird's-foot trefoil in spring and early summer to find the common blue butterfly, like a small piece of cut-out sky fallen to earth. Nettles are the sole food plant of red admiral, peacock and small tortoiseshell. The pink or whitish lady's smock or cuckoo flower that is widespread on damp ground on the island in spring is favoured by the little orange tip butterfly as well as the green-veined white.

Where nasturtiums grow in gardens or have strayed on to walls and road verges look out for the large and small white butterflies and the great variety of wild grasses on the island attract grayling, speckled wood, meadow brown, ringlet and the small heath. The scarcer dark green fritillary likes to lay its eggs on violets, and both dog and heath violets are widespread on Rathlin. Where there's sorrel – a common plant – you may find the small copper. Adult butterflies also need to feed, and flowers of many sorts attract them for the energy-giving nectar.

On a warm autumn day it is an amazing experience to watch red admiral and painted lady butterflies flying strongly along the coast and heading bravely out to sea, bound for the Mediterranean and Africa, fragile looking voyagers but skilled flyers and navigators – more than once I've murmured 'good luck' on witnessing such an emigration.

Flying Carpets

Those responsible for naming the moths have given them some intriguing labels: amongst the 18 or so carpet moths recorded on Rathlin (some rare) are the beautiful carpet, flame carpet, silver-ground carpet, blue-bordered carpet and chestnut-coloured carpet, which you will agree is a colourful range of flying carpets. In terms of names, add the small fan-footed wave, wormwood pug, scarce footman, autumnal rustic, mother shipton (showing an old-woman's face in its wing pattern) and many more and you realise that the moth-namers are not without imagination.

Those moth enthusiasts who travel to Rathlin and set up moth traps report much larger catches than on the mainland. Rathlin's variety of habitats and the long agricultural history of little pesticide or insecticide use is good news for moths. Many are root feeders and the healthy soils and plants aid their survival.

The moths studied at Rathlin – and over much of Northern Ireland – are the larger moths. There is a huge diversity of smaller species lumped under the term 'micro-moths' and they are not included here, being in the realm of the specialists. A fair number of moths are day-flying, but the majority are nocturnal and what we know of their occurrence is due to either moth-trapping (mostly with light-traps but also by providing tempting and boozy treats such as rum-flavoured treacle or a rope dipped in wine) or finds of moths clustering at other lights, notably light-houses and light-ships.

I have stood on the narrow platform that surrounds the lantern glass of a lighthouse on a murky and mild autumn night and seen enough moths lying dead or dazed around it to require a yard brush to clear them. That's not always the case, I'm glad to say, but the powerful beams of white light emitted by many lighthouses are ... well, you can imagine the effect on night-flying moths.

There were – when lighthouse-keepers were in residence before lights became automatic – a number of keepers who took part in voluntary recording schemes for migrating birds and moths. Reports of their findings added much to our knowledge of bird and moth migration but many lighthouses and lightships around Ireland did not host keepers with such an interest in recording projects, so we can only imagine what was missed.

A typical migrant moth and one I've seen in fair numbers at Rathlin, including amongst the revolving beams of the East Lighthouse, is the silver Y (no, not a typographical error, say it as 'silver why' rather than 'silvery'). It is fairly distinctive, the immigrants being a bit paler than the residents and both have a pale mark on each wing in the shape of the letter Y. This moth also flies in daylight.

Sometimes spectacular day-flying migration incidents take place, and masses of butterflies or moths may be seen including those out at sea spotted from islands and headlands and ships.

Butterfly and moth caterpillars form an important food item for many birds and even the adults, many being fast and agile flyers, are taken by some birds, notably the swift and the hobby, a falcon we don't see in Northern Ireland except on rare occasions. I've watched chaffinches catch moths amongst woodland and they are quite good at it. Bats are expert moth catchers.

Whether you're a birder or a botanist or someone with an eye for nature in general visiting Rathlin, it is worth keeping an eye out for the butterflies and moths – they add much to that buzz-word biodiversity and are a joy to watch.

8. FUR AND FEATHERS

Rathlin's terrestrial fauna is fascinating. By 'terrestrial fauna' I mean land mammals and land birds in general. The little creatures that fly and crawl and scrabble and often bite are in the realms of the entomologist and not being of this discipline, I don't have much to say about them. Scanning the limited natural history literature relating to Rathlin does not reveal much published, so if you are into bugs and littler things, Rathlin's the place to start hunting to add to the island's natural history archive. Moths, butterflies and dragonflies are already discussed.

Fascinating because on any island there are absences, intriguing presences, the problems of whether species arrived naturally or were introduced, the appearance and disappearance of genetic variations, and numbers matter – too many and the word pest comes to mind, too few and local extinction looms. So there are balances to study and explain. Islands are fascinating to naturalists.

Golden Hares and Mighty Mice

The Irish hare is a sub-species of the mountain hare of Northern Europe and differs a little from the Brown hare found in England and Wales. The history of these animals on Rathlin is intriguing. Hamilton reports in 1784: *"A few brace of hares indeed were lately introduced by the proprietor, which bid fair to produce a large increase."* This increase may have taken some time, as Marshall remarked on their scarcity in his 1837 paper. Catherine Gage (1851) lists hares as one of the island's mammals along with *"Norway rat, shrew mouse and common mouse"* from which we can safely assume she refers to the brown rat, the pygmy shrew and probably the house mouse. She mentions *"wild cats are said to formerly to have inhabited the white rocks beyond the church, living on mice, birds and eggs, but no trace of such animals can now be discovered."* Perhaps these were feral cats, still present on Rathlin, which have proved to be a problem for indigenous wildlife on some remote islands and difficult to eradicate. A recent example is the cat population on Tory Island off County Donegal, which has been subject to culling due to their taste for corncrakes; Tory being one of the few places in Ireland where these summer visitors still breed.

The Gages hosted guests and entertained many with shooting excursions. Hares continued to be shot, for both sport and food, and by the 1940s were reckoned to be at a very low level. New stock, I was told on the island, was introduced sometime in the 1950s and today there is a good population of hares. There is a genetic variation within Rathlin's population of hares which results in a beautiful gold coloured animal with pale blue eyes. As of 2011 there are at least two such golden hares on the island, much sought after by television wildlife film crews. They are not always easy to find.

These blue-eyed blondes are a *leucistic* type of the normally darker Irish hare, which means that they have a reduced amount of melanin, a substance that gives colour to animals. A complete absence of melanin leads to albino individuals which are all white, usually with pink eyes. These are rare inherited conditions, but in some isolated populations of island mammals, leucism can occur more often than would be expected in a larger collection of animals. For example, on Alderney in the

Channel Islands, up to 25% of the hedgehogs are blond. There is quite a lot of scientific debate about how these variations affect the creatures concerned: their eyesight, exposure to sunlight, how conspicuous they are to predators and so on. The hares on Rathlin are no longer shot and the adults – big animals – are probably too strong and heavy for a buzzard to cope with, although a golden or sea eagle could carry one off. From 1953 to 1961 a pair of golden eagles nested at Fair Head, no distance at all (for an eagle) from Rathlin, and the contents of their nest showed that adult hares were a regular feature of the food brought to the young, but these were said to be Scottish hares, not the Irish sub-species, so the eagles were probably doing some of their hunting across the channel, possibly at Kintyre or the islands of Jura and Islay. In May and early June, before these fields were cut, all I could see of the hares in the longer grasses was the tips of their ears, twitching and flicking. Hares are the most delightful animals to watch, and they have a major place in our folklore.

Rabbits came to Rathlin later than hares but exactly when I have been unable to trace. They were noted as absent by Hamilton in 1784 and Marshall did not mention them in the 1830s nor Gage in 1851. Islander Alex Morrison comments that rabbits were a welcome food when he was young (1920s and 1930s) but mentions their decline due to the later arrival of myxomatosis. Their population fluctuates and at present they are reasonably numerous but certainly not over-running the island. Rabbits form an important part of the diet of buzzards on Rathlin, and I have watched buzzards tearing young rabbits to bits and carrying off portions, probably to feed well grown nestlings.

There are no confirmed records of otters on Rathlin, although they occur on the mainland coast of County Antrim. There are no badgers or foxes, although the story goes (reported by Hamilton) that Lord Antrim, the landlord prior to the Gages leasing Rathlin from him in the 1740s, ordered his agent to bring some foxes to the island (probably to provide his Lordship and his guests with hunting sport) but the locals bribed him to take them away, and did so for some years, not wishing to have such a 'desolating invader' about the place. This did Rathlin's wildlife a favour, somewhat undone by the introduction of ferrets in the late 1980s.

Brown rats have existed on Rathlin for a long time – who knows when the first ones jumped ship and landed here? There is no evidence of them having any devastating effects on the island's birds or other wildlife, but on nearby Sheep Island rats wiped out the substantial puffin colony and by the 1970s only a handful were left. A sustained poisoning campaign by the National Trust in the late 1970s reduced the rat population considerably but the puffins did not survive. A successful programme using bait boxes with poisons eradicated brown rats on the Isle of Canna north of Rathlin, but too late to stop the rodents' genocide of Manx shearwaters (recent sightings raise hopes that they might re-establish there). Rathlin's ferrets, introduced in the 1980s, have proved, despite trapping, to be determined new residents. They could be enough, added to existing rats and feral cats, to threaten already vulnerable populations of ground-nesting birds and small mammals. The feasibility of eradication of rats and ferrets is currently (March 2011) being considered on the island, and increased bio-security may be necessary at the harbour and any other landing places to prevent any further introductions, accidental or deliberate.

The field mouse – also called the wood mouse - occurs on the island and sampling them in 1963 zoologist James Fairly noted that they were larger than mainland specimens. Most of the mice that he captured weighed in at 30 to 36 grammes, whereas a mainland mouse at 30 grams was considered chunky. On the Isle of Canna field mice turned the scales at nearly 34 grammes, and way up north on the St. Kilda Islands, there exist chubby ones of up to 40-50 grammes. Sub-species of field mice have been found on over a dozen islands up the west coast of Scotland and over to the Shetland Islands, in general considerably larger than mainland Scottish mice.

In general, large mammals on islands tend to get smaller (linked to food supplies) and small ones larger. A study of animals on many islands (quoted in Berry 2009), comparing them with mainland relatives found that, amongst rodents, six species had become smaller, one remained the same and 60 had increased in size.

The Rathlin field mice fit in with this pattern, although the sample was small. It doesn't seem to be climate, island size or remoteness that relate to this size discrepancy between mainland and island small mammals, but rather the absence of predation pressures. It would be interesting to know what effect, if any, the arrival of ferrets in the 1980s has had on Rathlin's field mice over the past couple of decades.

Wild Goats

There are a few wild goats living on Rathlin's exposed northern cliffs and slopes. They are probably more feral than truly wild, animals once domesticated that have escaped or been abandoned. I've watched some from a boat, making their way along a grassy cliff ledge high above the sea, impressive animals with broad, swept-back horns and shaggy grey fleeces. The leader of such social groups is invariably an old experienced nanny, and these animals also have horns.

Research on old wild Irish goats is hampered by a long history of their genes being mixed with those of a domestic/feral origin. Nevertheless, there may have been truly wild goats roaming Ireland thousands of years ago after the last Ice Age. There are unknown numbers of 'wild' goats scattered about Ireland, including groups on offshore islands like Rathlin.

Bats

Bats occur on the island but, despite requests to several organisations, I've received no information. The brown long-eared bat is present, and I've seen pipistrelle bats hunting around some old buildings but am not sure which species (three are known to occur in Northern Ireland).

Land Birds

The birds of Rathlin are many and varied, with the island's good position for receiving migrants adding to the island's bird list.

The Gage family of Rathlin took a great interest in natural history (see the chapter on naturalists) and Catherine Gage's 1851 book gives a list of island birds known up to that year, totalling about 92 species. Patterson's paper of 1892 mentions 123 species. In 1960, 175 species were located, with 79 breeding; now (2010) at least 190 are on the list of which about 80 are known to breed.

No doubt there are other lists but these give an idea of the island's known avifauna over the past 160 years. The changes may be attributed in part to more observers, a growing list of migrants, species protection and habitat fluctuations.

The seabirds are treated separately, so what follows is about land birds, (fresh-water birds and shore birds are mentioned in the wetlands section).

One of Rathlin's star birds is the chough. There is a single breeding pair (2010) and these are the only choughs to be found in all of Northern Ireland. Thus they have extreme rarity status and these two birds and their occasional offspring are a sad reminder that the chough was once the commonest crow on Rathlin. Common in terms of numbers, for I always think of the chough as a bit of an aristocrat amongst birds: the ringing call, the blue-black glossy plumage, the broad feather-fingered wings, the buoyant flight with soaring, gliding and swooping, the bright red legs and feet and curved red beak of a fine nature, used like two lacquered and bent chopsticks to winkle insects from soil and crevices – all these features make the chough a unique crow and a joy to watch.

Marshall, visiting Rathlin in the 1830s, wrote:

"In the month of July I found them everywhere, associated in large flocks, at one place frequenting inland situations, and at another congregated on the sea-shore. They had just collected together their different families, now fully fledged, and were picking up their food (which consisted chiefly of insects) either on the shore, or in the crevices of rocks, or in the pasture fields."

These are astute observations and studies since then have confirmed how post-breeding chough families gather just as Marshall described, and that such social flocking seems to be important in chough life.

In west Donegal such gatherings are often found on short-cropped turf amongst sand dunes, giving rise to the local name of 'warren crow'. Where the lonely Rathlin birds go to socialise is not known, but colour-ringing them in recent years may answer this question. The nearest chough populations are in north Donegal and over on the island of Islay in Scotland. Catherine Gage wrote of the chough in 1851: *"This handsome bird is by far the most numerous species of crow on the island."* Robert Patterson's study of Rathlin's birds (1892) describes them as: *"very common all over the island."* Naturalists visiting Rathlin throughout the first half of the twentieth century noted choughs to be reasonably plentiful, although Edward Armstrong in 1940 writes that: *"The choughs are much less in number than they used to be."* He described how collectors sought their eggs and referred to them as 'persecuted'. Nevertheless, he enjoyed watching a flock of fifteen.

In 1960 and 1961, when we ran the bird observatory on Rathlin's southern arm (East Light to Rue Point), daily counts in August and

September 1960 recorded 12 to 20 choughs regularly while in 1961 up to 14 were seen in April and May and in September the maximum daily count was 22. At this time, choughs were also present as breeding birds along the Antrim coast from near Torr Head to the Giant's Causeway and occasionally as far west as the Downhill cliffs in Co. Londonderry. In the late 1970s on Rathlin five pairs were breeding and it was still possible to see up to 24 in a summer flock. Subsequent surveys showed, however, that they declined steadily through the 1980s and 1990s on both Rathlin and the mainland to the single pair left at present. Intensive farming along the cliff tops with use of pesticides and insecticides was identified as the most likely cause of this decline on the mainland, for the chough seeks its insects in short turf and amongst cliff vegetation as well as searching cow pats for flies and their larvae. Why they declined on Rathlin, where farming has been more environmentally friendly, is a bit of a mystery. There is a record of one bird being shot, but in general they have not been persecuted in recent decades. Peregrines are known to prey on choughs at times, but Rathlin's peregrines have a wide choice of feeding, such as rock doves (favourite prey for some of these falcons), the masses of summer seabirds and plenty of starlings and smaller prey.

Due to the bird's disappearance from mainland Northern Ireland, Rathlin's breeding choughs are now celebrities and let us hope they don't, as celebrities are inclined to, fade away and vanish.

Arrivals and Departures

As soon as this book is published it will be out of date, at least in terms of the island's fauna. Change happens quickly on small islands - boundaries are limited and, seabirds apart, many populations are considerably smaller than on the mainland. New birds, especially migrants, will be added to the list.

The status of the Manx shearwater as a breeding bird is uncertain yet the first full survey of the island's seabirds in 1969 estimated it as quite numerous, maybe as many as 1000 pairs.

Eagles are a good example of arrivals and departures. The eagle mentioned by nineteenth century naturalists (Thompson 1849, Gage 1851, Patterson 1892) is the sea eagle (also called the white-tailed eagle). Patterson wrote in 1892:

> *"This bird was formerly a constant resident, and bred in the rocks on the north side of the island, but owing to the havoc it committed on young lambs it was shot down and the nests robbed. It has not been seen for some years."*

The last surviving nesting pair may have been those mentioned by Thompson in 1849. Golden eagles were uncommon, even rare, visitors although the Fair Head pair must have passed over regularly in the 1950s. Sea eagles have been successfully re-introduced to western Scotland and golden eagles similarly to Donegal, so it's not surprising that occasional individuals of these two species have been seen on Rathlin in recent years and perhaps their occurrences will increase, although probably only as visiting birds.

The corncrake declined in Ireland from being an abundant summer resident, probably numbering tens of thousands prior to the 1960s, to 129 calling birds in a 1994 survey. Changes in agricultural practices have been blamed, such as the loss of hay meadows to intensive silage swards cut two or three times a year, as well as an increase in sheep which kept marginal vegetation grazed down, reducing early season cover for these birds. Conservation work has helped to keep the remaining 127 calling birds (2009) relatively stable in a few core areas where they still exist. The corncrake is a recent loss on Rathlin. *"Very frequent in the corn fields and meadows,"* wrote Catherine Gage in 1851, a comment echoed by Patterson in 1892 who noted April 27th as the earliest date it was heard. The bird observatory work in 1961 showed that the first corncrake arrived on 21 April and thereafter birds were heard calling almost daily, with six to 10 regularly noted in May. This was only on the N-S arm of the island – more would have been present on the E-W arm. By 1979 there were only four or five calling and by 1988, when an all-Ireland survey took place, not one was heard, although a few birds did come and go into the 1990s; the last recorded breeding pair was in 1997 and calling birds were noted in 1998 and 2004. Despite attempts to manage suitable habitat (early season shelter such as clumps of yellow flag iris shoots and nettles and areas of long grasses in summer) it has not yet re-established. The corncrake has become one of Rathlin's spirits – the ghost in the meadows.

An exciting arrival has been a pair of great skuas which visited the western moorlands for a year or two and nested in 2010 but apparently the hatched chicks did not survive. Nesting was also recorded in the same year in County Mayo. This big, aggressive seabird is not easily intimidated and may try again to establish itself on Rathlin. It nests in good numbers in the Outer Hebrides, Orkney and Shetland.

The changing fortunes of the seabirds may see departures in terms of numbers but hopefully not of species, at least not immediately. The Manx shearwater situation remains uncertain. Terns no longer breed on Rathlin but they are fickle in their loyalties to nesting areas and could return. Cormorants have come and gone – another colonial breeder that can rise and fall relatively quickly in terms of numbers.

Little Brown Jobs

Birders have an acronym for all those small and mousey-coloured birds that do not stand out; they call them 'LBJs', or 'Little Brown Jobs'. When Rathlin had a human population of over 1000 (1780s to 1840s) and much more of the land was tilled for grain crops, the corn bunting must have been resident, and Gage mentions it in her 1851 list. This streaky buff and brown bird declares its presence with a metallic little song, likened by some to the jingling of a bunch of keys. It is absent now as breeding bird (from Rathlin and the rest of Northern Ireland), not surprisingly as tilled land is very scarce as pasture and hay and silage grasses now dominate the island's agricultural landscape, as they do throughout Ireland's farmlands. The planting of coniferous trees in the 1950s and their slow and somewhat uneven growth has provided habitats for a number of small birds and long-eared owls.

The rough grasslands and heaths are home to moderate numbers of skylarks and it is a pleasure to walk and cycle about the island and be serenaded from March to July by these songsters. More intensively managed grasslands, cut up to three times a season for silage, have greatly reduced their breeding habitats and hence numbers in many parts of Northern Ireland. In spring and early summer, little brown meadow pipits perform a fluttering song flight, rising into the air and singing as they descend, and you might think they are unskilled skylarks, but their song trills down the scale and lacks the vigour of the lark. You have to admire them for trying.

Claws

Birds of prey are often seen on Rathlin. Peregrine falcons nest on the high cliffs, as do buzzards, and both sparrowhawk and kestrel also breed. All four are resident throughout the year and the most obvious is the broad-winged buzzard, drifting high over your head or cruising lower down over the fields and heaths looking for young rabbits, birds, even frogs. Peregrines feed almost exclusively on birds, favouring rock doves and the occasional auk or kittiwake or snatching a starling from summer flocks, one of the fastest birds in the world when dropping like a stone out of the sky in what is called a 'stoop' to strike its prey at over 160 km per hour (100 miles per hour). The sparrowhawk is another bird hunter, its main hunting tactic being surprise, sweeping over a hedge or wall to snatch a small bird from a flock or, using its great flying agility, weaving through woodland or scrub in pursuit of its prey. Kestrels hover, and can spot mice and even beetles from quite a height, dropping into the vegetation to grab whatever they see. The dashing merlin, a small falcon about the size of a mistle thrush, is a regular autumn and winter visitor. Rarer birds of prey recorded at Rathlin include red kite, hen harrier, marsh harrier, rough-legged buzzard, hobby, gyr falcon, snowy owl and booted eagle, while the barn owl – once a scarce resident - seems to have gone.

If you have followed this nature tour, and dipped into the other chapters, you will realise that Rathlin, despite its exposed position and rugged appearance, has a small but interesting array of land mammals and a wealth of bird life. The island is particularly blessed in spring and summer when the seabirds are clamouring and whizzing about the cliffs and rock stacks, and they share the coastal and offshore waters with marine mammals such as seals, whales, dolphins and porpoises. It is time to go down to the sea, which is never far away on Rathlin.

9. THE WATER MARGIN

The Seashores

Rathlin has a coastline of 30 km (18 miles), all of it rocky except for a narrow crescent of sand in the inner part of Church Bay from the harbour to the old quay. Most of what we would call seashore – leaving aside sandy beaches – can be found on the island from the white cliffs to the south side of Church Bay and on the east coast: rock pools, stones and boulders covered with seaweed, similarly clad rock shelves and crevices and patches of shingle. Most of the rest of Rathlin's shores are very exposed and difficult to get to, except by steep scrambles or using a small boat in calm weather. There are some rocky and boulder-strewn bays at the western end, guarded by high cliffs, and many small coves with rocky shore platforms and boulder or cobble beaches that are below high cliffs and out of reach of all but the most determined beach comber. Many of the sea caves have boulder or stony beaches and rocky ledges inside them, the haunts of moaning seals and nesting shags.

Some of Rathlin's children can a few metres from their front door explore the pools, shelves, crevices and overhangs of the chalk bedrock and chalk and basalt stones around the shores of Church Bay. Here, slipping and sliding on all kinds of green, brown and red seaweeds, they can discover lots of clinging, scrabbling, nipping and swimming things. Poking a pencil (or a finger if you are braver) into the tentacles of a large sea anemone and feeling that most gentle sucking tug is just one step towards a lifelong fascination with the seashore.

First, a few words about boulders, stones and sand. Those who study shores and seabeds classify these according to size, by actual diameter in millimetres to be exact. Without giving figures, these are, in descending size: boulders; cobbles (rounded stones); pebbles; gravels; coarse sand; medium sand; fine sand and mud. A general rule of thumb would be: if you can't lift it, it's bedrock or boulder, if you can, its anything from cobble to gravel, if it makes castles it's sand and if you get stuck in it, it's mud (or quicksand).

Like my unscientific classification above, my own kit for exploring the seashore is simple – shorts and sandals (in summer, anyhow, welly boots in winter but they slip terribly and fill with water at a moment's notice), a sturdy long-handled net of fine mesh, a white plastic tray about 5 cm (2 ins) deep to release catches into and examine, a small hand lens of about 10X or 20X magnification and a good field guide to seashore plants and animals. Oh, and maybe a towel as it's easy to fall in. Two final comments on seashore exploring - always put things back as you found them, be they living organisms, or stones you have over-turned or seaweeds pulled aside, and as for health and safety, use common sense and be aware of tides and waves.

Surveys and Science

The first detailed examination of Rathlin's inter-tidal areas – the littoral zone – was carried out by a team from Edinburgh's Heriot-Watt University during a survey of all of Northern Ireland's shorelines in 1984-88. A total of 14 rocky sites around the island produced enough information to enable a later evaluation (2002) to recommend areas worthy of conservation designation and protection. In 2005, by which time these recommendations had been acted upon, marine biologists from the Northern Ireland Environment Agency (part of the Department of the Environment) re-surveyed a selection of the above 14 sites. The following is based on the above work and my own explorations in the field.

Rathlin's rocky shores – like those around the rest of Britain and Ireland and elsewhere – show zonations of typical plants and animals from the very top of the shore splashed by waves and spray down to the lowest parts exposed at extreme spring tides. Sometimes these zones can be very narrow, as on cliff-bound or very steep shorelines, and at the other extreme they can extend a long way across gently shelving or almost flat shores. The tidal range – the amount of rise and fall between high and low tides – has a large influence on the inter-tidal areas exposed, and on the life that exists there. Around Rathlin, the tidal range is small, generally about 1.5 metres (5 feet) although tidal streams are strong.

The 1980s littoral survey identified five main shore types around Rathlin. These are (I've paraphrased them somewhat):

1. Very exposed areas with barnacles, limpets, the long-fronded brownish-green seaweed known as 'dabberlocks' and the small reddish Corallina weed which is much branched and feels quite hard due to its chalky bead-like structure.

2. Less steep exposed shores with some sheltered areas and long straps of thong weed showing at low tide (not to be confused with the coils of more rounded bootlace weed that lie just offshore around many of the island's shores).

3. Moderately exposed shores of bedrock and boulders with common brown seaweeds such as bladder wrack and saw wrack, black lichens coating the rocks and purplish filmy seaweed known as Porphyra.

4. Sheltered shores with boulders and typical zonations of brown and red seaweeds from the upper to the lower shore.

5. Cave sites with tidally exposed ledges and boulder beaches.

Within these shore types, combinations of the physical habitats and recurring community types of plants and animals are known as *biotopes*. On Rathlin, 25 such biotopes have so far been identified around the shores. Most of us, with a little practice, could recognise the shore types; knowing the biotopes requires rather more knowledge and expertise. These are, nevertheless, important categories for marine biologists and ecologists to make sense of the complex array of habitats, plants and animals around our shores (and on land). The identification of 25 biotopes is an indicator that Rathlin, when examined closely, is more diverse in seashore life than you might think at first glance.

The above classifications tend to rely on relatively static features – rocky structures, aspect, steepness, rocks with lichens, barnacles and limpets, seaweeds types and zones. The more active and mobile creatures that move about the shore, sometimes crossing the various zones, are what add the spice to rock-pooling and shore explorations.

Neptune's Sweetie Jar

When you dip into the clear waters of Rathlin's rock pools and poke about other parts of the shoreline, you find many small and colourful things. Under the thick coating of seaweeds hides the painted top shell, a markedly conical red and pink mollusc. This, and other similar shells, might sometimes harbour a hermit crab. Scuttling about below the weed and in rock pools are the green and brown shore crabs and the greyish fuzzy-backed velvet crab which has beautiful bluish-purple marks on its legs and claws. Starfish on the shore are usually the medium-sized straw-coloured common starfish and little stubby cushion stars, varying from grey to yellowish to red. If you are lucky, a vivid red and orange sunstar might turn up, usually a smallish one, with twelve 'arms' rather than the five found on the above. To see a sea slug glide across a rock is a real treat, for these can be very colourful with side frills marked like a Spanish dancer's dress. Sea anemones of red, blue, yellow, green and purple occur in pools and under crevices, especially lower down the shore, and it is always worth parting the big brown seaweeds at the edge of the reefs at low tide to see what might be there.

Fish of various shapes and colours dart about the pools. The blennies are an interesting group, small fish that are smooth and slippery to the feel as they have no scales. The green and brown common blenny has the endearing habit of resting on top of a rock and peering at you, the large eyes and rather pouting mouth giving it a permanent surprised expression. It can survive out of the water beneath seaweed or under rocks for several hours, as long as its skin is moist enough for oxygen to be absorbed. A reddish long bodied fish with a number of whisker-like growths about the head and mouth may slither away from you, a three-bearded or shore rockling. One of the most vividly hued creatures to be spotted is the spiny squat lobster, about finger length or a little larger, found under heavy weed growth or in crevices. It is a type of small lobster, with long front claws. This little animal is bright orange, marked with the most startling lapis-lazuli blue.

All the above plus lemon and orange periwinkles, green breadcrumb sponge and vivid orange and yellow lichens on the rocks (not together – the lichens at the top of the shore, the sponges live further down nearer the sea) and more make pottering about Rathlin's shores an endlessly fascinating activity. When the tide goes out, we can dip into Neptune's sweetie jar and marvel at the contents – but don't put any of them in your mouth!

KELP

Fires on the Shore

Rathlin wears a thick skirt of seaweeds. At low tide, these brown and red sea-algae hang in damp fronds from the base of cliffs and large boulders, and glistening stalks and shiny broad fingers move back and forth in the surge beyond the lower shores. At high tide, they become tall shady forests in the clear waters around the island, havens for fish and shellfish and other marine life. Closer to the shore, the bladder wracks (wrack is a general term for many of these inshore seaweeds) float buoyed up by their numerous air sacs and great coils of bootlace weed make patterns on the surface, like curls of mermaid's hair. Between the tides, brown and red seaweeds often form dense coverings on the bedrock and boulders.

Today, divers explore the kelp forests and shore anglers despair as their shiny and expensive lures catch on these tough stems and fronds making their lines break. Nobody pays much attention to the great banks of seaweed washed ashore in winter and spring, unless they happen to appear on an amenity beach where local authorities send tractors and automated rakes to gather it all up, depriving birds of the rich insect harvest that might otherwise offend fastidious humans who prefer long stretches of clean white sands.

It was very different a couple of hundred years ago. In the 1700s and 1800s, island and mainland coastal dwelling communities of the western and northern shores of Ireland (and Scotland) laboured in a sustainable if arduous industry to make kelp. The word 'kelp' has two meanings: it is often used to describe the living fringe of seaweeds, usually of the larger brown and red varieties, in our temperate coastal waters while an older use of the word was to describe the produce of dried and burned seaweeds, a blue-black, heavy, congealed mass of rock hard substance rich in useful chemicals. This was the kelp of the kelp industry, beginning in the 1700s and running through the 1800s to finally die out in the 1930s and 1940s as other, larger and more easily obtained sources of potash and iodine – to name two of the most useful products from kelp – became available.

Travellers to Rathlin, the Glens of Antrim and the Causeway Coast in the above period could not fail to notice the great plumes of whitish smoke from fires on the shores. Many drawings and paintings from those times show such clouds of smoke and there are written accounts of sweating, sooty-faced men, women and children toiling at the kelp kilns. Tales of kelp work are included in the Folklore section. Gathering the seaweed, carrying it to the drying walls and then burning it was a back-breaking, dirty and sometimes dangerous job, but this seasonal work provided substantial proportions of a family's annual income, put alongside fishing and farming.

In 1784, William Hamilton noted that 100 tons of kelp was produced on Rathlin that year, fetching five pounds five shillings per ton (five pounds 25p). The £525 raised was almost enough to clear the £600 annual rent due to the landlord. To produce 100 tons of kelp required a great deal of work. With such good resources growing close to the island, a lot of the weed was cut by hand, the gatherers either wading into the sea or working from boats, using sharp cutters attached to poles. Others collected what was washed ashore by winter gales and even as late as May, when the cuckoo-storms of that month threw up the 'May fleece', the last of the old die-back of winter weed. This heavy wet harvest had to be carried in creels woven from willow and hazel rods up cliff tracks and over boulder shores to specially built low kelp drying walls. Here it was stacked to dry before being burned in pit kilns, long troughs lined with stones. It could take 24 to 36 hours to burn a kiln-full down to the sticky residue that cooled and hardened into kelp.

Estimates vary, but one fisherman who gathered seaweed for kelp at Dunseverick (on the coast opposite Rathlin) over the period 1928 to 1936 told me (in 1984) it took at least 10 tons of wet weed to yield a ton of kelp, sometimes nearly twice that, depending on the type of seaweed gathered. As an example, he said they opened up their kelp kiln at 4am on a Friday morning and burned continuously until 4pm on Saturday, then left it to cool and harden before breaking it up into smaller pieces and bagging it for the agent to collect. They received about £5 per ton (much as the Rathlin islanders did almost 150 years earlier in 1784) and their best production in that period was 10 tons in one year at £8 per ton, the £80 raised being half their annual income (from fishing and kelp).

The landlords at Rathlin over the years of the kelp boom were Robert Gage senior and his son Robert junior, spanning the period 1739-1862. They allocated the island's shores to tenants at a shore rent of £2 per allocation per year and, as stated above, took the kelp profits towards annual rents due. In the western seaboard of Scotland about this time, some landlords became richer from their tenants' kelp production, raising as much as 55% profit. At Rathlin, any resentment that may have simmered was tempered by the landlord's management of the kelp industry, providing a substantial and dry kelp store – essential as rain could leach out the valuable salts in the kelp - and assistance with marketing. After the landlord's control waned in the 1930s, the islanders' kelp was sold directly to the shippers and low prices gradually discouraged production (McCurdy, 2010).

In the mid-1800s there were 150 kelp kilns on Rathlin and in the 1950s islanders could remember (probably back to the early 1900s) 50 in operation. A recent survey (reported in 2006) by maritime archaeologists found remains of 83 kilns around the island's shores, as well as old kelp walls and other bits and pieces of the industry. It should be remembered that in Hamilton's time there were around 1200 people living on Rathlin, and kelp was therefore an important island industry – probably the only one capable of boosting incomes for a population whose subsistence was otherwise dependent on fishing and farming and a bit of weaving.

The uses to which kelp products were put have helped to classify kelp production into periods: 1700 to 1820 was the alkali period, when the alkaline potashes were used for bleaching, making soap and glass and in paper-making and in alum which was used in dyes; as alternative sources for potashes began to be used. The discovery of iodine in kelp residues in 1811 renewed the kelp industry as iodine was important both as a medicine and in photographic processes, thus the iodine period extended from 1820 to 1940. By the 1940s kelp products were replaced by other sources of these chemicals, and only the production of alginates – gels from the seaweeds useful in cosmetic and foods – has kept a seaweed industry going to date, mainly in the west of Ireland.

Most of the available seaweeds were used in Rathlin's kelp industry. The large brown algae that grow beyond low water mark – those of the *Laminaria* group – were popular and their thick stems, known as 'rods' were used as much as the fronds. The brown *Fucus* seaweeds such as bladder wrack and saw or toothed wrack were also collected and another weed taken in particular at Rathlin was *Chorda filum*, in places known as 'bootlace weed' or 'dead-man's rope', which is abundant around the southern shores of the island. Red weeds, often found growing on the stems of the large Laminaria, were included in the collections.

Today, the shell of the large kelp store, built of limestone (chalk) blocks, is a conspicuous feature in Church Bay. Less obvious but numerous are the low kelp walls and partially over-grown kelp kilns clustered about the shores close to the upper tide mark, but they are there nevertheless, a reminder of a time when there were lots of islanders toiling at the fires on the shore.

Only the wrack and ruins remain.

10. THE SURROUNDING SEA

Hubble Bubble, Tides and Trouble

If you live on an island, the sea that surrounds you is of great importance. It influences the weather, is the highway for ship traffic, provides food and even shapes the very home you depend on through erosion by the waves. The salty winds affect what you can grow, including trees, and the sea's tides, currents, temperatures and salinities (water saltiness), as well as the waves generated, influence the plants and animals found on the shores and under the water. Islanders get to know their surrounding sea in detail, mostly through day-to-day experiences.

Anyone who sails in Rathlin's waters or otherwise travels by small boat in the area will tell you that the island's tides are complicated, dangerous and need watching. There are various tides and eddies around Rathlin, each with its own name and reputation, and a folklore has built up around these, as discussed later in this book.

Rathlin's position is significant, the Atlantic Ocean battering its western shores and the North Channel sweeping in from the east. The waters swirl and race twice a day around the island as the tides rise and fall. The ebb tide runs generally west through the North Channel and when it turns to the flood, the flow is eastwards. That seems simple enough, but the presence of Rathlin leads to all sorts of complex tidal movements and timings around the islands coasts. Wallace Clark, author of a book on Rathlin and a lifelong sailor with intimate knowledge of the these waters, describes the complexity of the tidal movements as causing streams, counter-streams, hollow troughs, pyramid waves and advises that it takes a lifetime of experience to know Rathlin's seven tides. I've been all around the island and offshore in fishing boats, mostly rather small, and felt the power of the tide races and had spray in my face and green water soak me. In September 1973, trying to recover experimental lobster pots set off-shore at the Middle Bank between Rathlin and Islay, we watched in amazement the tide race pull below the surface a 250 litre (55 gallon) empty oil drum we were using as a float, and smelled the friction burning of polypropylene ropes on the winch as we tried to haul a line of pots against this tide.

With these powerful tidal streams around the island, one might expect equally dramatic rises and falls of tide between high and low water. The opposite is true, the tidal range at Rathlin being around 1.5 metres (5 ft), while to the south at Strangford Lough it is 4 metres (13 ft). This is due to a phenomenon known as an *amphidromic point*, situated just south of Islay off Rathlin's north side. This is a calculated point, not something you can see such as a headland. If you swirl water around vigorously in a deep bowl, you will notice it rising and falling considerably at the rim but there is little or no movement in the centre. Tides oscillate like this around a centre or amphidromic point. Rathlin's location at such a locus explains the small tidal range; the island is – so to speak – at the centre of the bowl.

Cool and Cooler Running Water

If you swim at Rathlin without a wet-suit, you will discover why this sub-heading does not read 'hot and cold running water'. The average near surface temperatures are around seven degrees centigrade in winter and about 13.5 degrees in summer so the sea does not freeze but neither does it warm much; the salinity remains fairly constant at 34.25 grams of salt per kilogram of total dissolved salt (that's equivalent to 3.4% saltiness); significant wave heights (wave height exceeded for 10% of the time) are 1.5 metres in summer and 2.5 metres in winter. These heights are averages, which smooth things out, and you can experience much higher waves at times around Rathlin. All this is complex enough without adding non-metric measurements – you can look these up if required.

Enough statistics, what does all this mean? It means that the sea surrounding Rathlin is anything but a flat and uninteresting expanse of water. The recently gained knowledge of the detailed topography of the sea bed around the island as shown by multi-beam sonar mapping will allow more accurate interpretation of how sea bottom ridges, troughs, mounds, pinnacles and the like affect tides, currents, waves and the rest, but many marine animals are very aware of the tiniest changes in any of the factors outlined above.

11. UNDER THE WAVES

From Dredgers to Divers

*"Encouraged by the success of our last year's work, four of our party
determined to dredge again in Church Bay, Rathlin Island..."*

George Chaster was an enthusiast for marine molluscs, mainly the
seashells and their living inhabitants. He wrote the above in his paper
reporting a trip to Rathlin in 1897, when their small sailing vessel was
becalmed and the boatman decided not to risk exposure to the strong
tidal race beyond the shelter of Church Bay. So they made the best of
it and managed to add one new species to the British and Irish marine
molluscan fauna.

In the time before the development of modern diving technology,
Chaster and his colleagues had no option but to explore the seabed by
dragging a dredge behind a boat and sieving the sand and other
sediments from the contents to retrieve their catch. During sea trips
around Rathlin and off the north coast of Ireland in 1970-75, I used
similar techniques to survey *benthic* (sea bed) fauna but at least we had
a powerful trawler fitted with winches and navigation aids.

A number of incidents in the early 1970s led me to suspect that
underwater, Rathlin might be full of surprises. We watched a northern
bottlenose whale leap from the sea twice as it followed the edge of the
deeps off the north coast of the island; we shook a strange small fish
out of a lobster pot hauled from almost 130 metres (over 400 feet) off
the north-western cliffs, a rare Yarrell's blenny; big yellowish fan mussels

turned up in dredges west of the island, and one close to the coast; seabirds in great numbers plunged and dived in the turbulent island waters seeking plankton and small fish while divers of the time told stories of underwater cliffs, caves and shipwrecks festooned with life.

In 2007, over one hundred years after Chaster's dredging expeditions to Rathlin, and thirty-five years after mine, a SCUBA (Self-Contained Underwater Breathing Apparatus) diving survey at the island reported 128 types of sponges, eight of them new to science, bringing Rathlin's total for marine sponges to 134 species.

Other diving investigations and the use of Remotely Operated Vehicles (ROVs) fitted with cameras have revealed that the underwater environment of Rathlin is rich enough in marine life to be recognised as a nationally important 'hotspot' for marine flora and fauna. Multi-beam sonar surveys of the area, mentioned earlier, have revealed physical details of the seabed far beyond the results charted by Victorian hydrographers wielding lead lines and fixing their positions by sextant. Chaster would be amazed.

The Madding Crowd

Life underwater in some ways is similar to that on land: it's a struggle for space and food, and in the case of plants, also for light. At Rathlin, from the seashore into the depths, every boulder, every rock face, even the artificial reefs of decaying shipwrecks provide surfaces for seaweeds to fasten to (where there is enough light), for soft corals, sponges, sea anemones and more to encrust and in the shelter of boulders, crevices and sea caves lurk conger eels, one of over 30 species of fish, as well as nippers and creepers such as lobsters, squat lobsters and crabs. In shallower water and at moderate depths, the edges of reefs and cliffs are swept by tidal streams and strong currents, bringing a varied menu of food in the form of clouds of tiny plants and animals of the plankton. Deeper down, a snowfall of edible debris and the day/night downward and upward migrations of larger plankton also help to fill the water column with food for all these entangling, stinging, filtering, sucking and grabbing creatures that live out most of their lives either attached to something, lurking and waiting or actively hunting. Even far beyond the last glimmers of light from above, in the dark cold depths at 200 metres and more (over 650 ft), there are encrusting, burrowing and swimming things, many of them extremely colourful.

Endless Forms Most Beautiful and Most Wonderful...

Charles Darwin closed his famous book *On The Origin of Species* (1859) with these words, referring to both past and continuing evolution. He could well have been writing of Rathlin's undersea life.

The first detailed Scuba diving survey of Rathlin's sub-tidal flora and fauna was carried out 1983-85 by staff of the Ulster Museum, under contract to the Department of the Environment for Northern Ireland. This was part of a diving exploration of the inshore waters around all of Northern Ireland (1982-86). Divers surveyed 148 sites around the island in depths from two to 48 metres (six to 157 feet). A total of 530 species of plants and animals found under the waves at Rathlin represented 62% of the total tally of species in the whole Northern Ireland survey. This put Rathlin 'on the map' not only in terms of regional importance but nationally as well, the massive underwater cliffs off the north-western and northern areas proving unique in terms of habitat and life throughout the United Kingdom and Ireland.

Colourful assemblages of seaweeds, sponges, sea squirts and much more came to light, literally, as the divers shone powerful beams on to cliff faces and into rocky crevices and sub-marine caves and explored boulder fields, sand and gravel beds, kelp forests and some of the many shipwreck remains that are scattered around Rathlin's dangerous coast. The crawfish was seen amongst rocky areas off the north-west coast, where we'd caught the occasional specimen using barrel pots in deep water. This first detailed survey highlighted the variety of underwater habitats, the great diversity of species, the presence of several rarities and seaweed growth in the clear waters down to depths of 20 metres (65 ft).

All of this information was used to make cases for conservation designations such as *Areas of Special Scientific Interest* (ASSI) and *Special Area of Conservation* (SAC), protective listings which now apply to Rathlin's coastline and its underwater environment to between one and two km (0.8 to 1.25 miles) offshore.

Marine biologists are familiar with the scientific names of the plants and animals they observe, but that does not stop them giving English names to some of these, many of which are very descriptive and imaginative. At Rathlin, we have the *prawn cracker, crumpled duster* and *breadcrumb sponges,* the *light bulb sea squirt* and the *fluted squirt,* the *helter-skelter hydroid, Christmas tree sea slug, reticulated dragonet* (a fish) and *cuckoo wrasse* (another fish). Even the seaweeds can have evocative names, such as *dabberlocks* and *furbelows,* two of the larger brown algae of the lower shore and inshore waters.

Divers, both amateur and professional, have assembled a great deal of data on Rathlin's underwater life in the past decade. The following is based on field work up to and including 2009 and survey reports to 2011, kindly provided by the Northern Ireland Environment Agency's diving team and those from the Ulster Museum, plus surveys carried out through a voluntary recording scheme known as Seasearch. Sources of information are acknowledged in the references.

An Underwater Tour

As the ferry enters the broad reach of Church Bay you are passing over a seabed that is largely sand and shell and pebbles, where *sea cucumbers, heart urchins* and *brittle starfish* are typical residents. This is also the only location in Northern Ireland, near the white cliffs, where the *spotted burrowing sea anemone* occurs, enough of them to make this site a United Kingdom stronghold for this delicate and lovely creature. Various key species of starfishes, hermit crab, sea pen and sea slugs are further evidence that these softer seabed areas are an important habitat. Recent findings of distinctive deep burrows suggest the presence of the eel-like *red band fish*, more usually found in the soft and sticky mud of the Irish Sea.

Further west, past the end of the white cliffs, the shore drops steeply underwater to 70 metres (230 ft) and a boulder strewn seabed here is rich in sponges, some of them rare species, and a similar fauna occurs on submarine chalk cliffs below Bull Point at the far west corner of Rathlin.

At this western end of the island and round to the north-western cliff-bound side, passing the West Lighthouse perched on a ledge like a man whose hat has blown off (the lantern house is at the bottom of the lighthouse tower), the underwater environment is a mix of eroded and pitted chalk cliff faces and ledges, basalt rock faces, archways, gullies and sea caves. These are all covered with sponges, soft corals such as *deadman's fingers*, clusters of bright yellow anemones, indeed, almost every marine life form you could think of is represented. Some of the pitted chalk faces are dotted with hundreds of small and colourful *Devonshire cup corals*, making this look, as one diver described it to me, like someone had scattered little sweets everywhere.

Passing round towards the northern coast, there are awesome (the only word, even if it is over-used) underwater cliffs that drop like huge walls to depths of 224 metres (730 ft) just a short distance offshore. Closer in, at the upper part of one of these walls known as *Duncan's Bo* (on Rathlin, *bo* means a reef, a word derived from the Norse language), life is more patchy as strong currents and eddies diverted by nearby headlands sweep away all but the most clinging organisms. Sea caves have been reported here at depths over 60 metres (almost 200 feet), some as yet to be explored.

North-west of these cliffs, at one of the deepest sites so far examined, by a ROV with cameras attached, amongst broken rock at 224 metres (730 ft), *peacock worms* were discovered, probably finding anchor points in the sediments trapped between the rocks. Each of these beautiful animals, normally found on muddy sea beds, extrudes a brightly coloured fan of fine tentacles to intercept tiny food organisms.

The sea floor off Rathlin's east coast is more sloping, with extensive areas of boulders and cobbles (smaller rounded boulders or large stones), some areas of sand also with boulders and rocky reefs. There is a rare example of a *maerl bed*, 'maerl' being colourful twig-like pieces of a type of seaweed with a hard chalky covering making them look like little bits of broken coral. The boulders support many red seaweeds and are a good habitat for brown crabs and lobsters, including vulnerable young lobsters that need shelter from predators. Many of the hydroids known as *sea-firs* live here, beautifully coloured and delicate and several species rare in Northern Ireland waters have been identified.

The rusting structure of the troop carrier *Lochgarry* lies at 34 metres (110 ft) depth a short distance off this east coast. Every bit of available space on this artificial reef is covered with marine organisms, and fish swim through its skeleton, notably colourful wrasse, large pollack and ling (the last two members of the cod family). The ship sank in a storm in 1942 (29 lives lost, 30 saved) and in its almost 70 years lying upright on the seabed has become a home for new life and a popular dive site.

This has been a rather general tour of Rathlin's underwater riches but enough, I hope, to show what an amazing world exists under the waves. To do this world justice would require an entire book, indeed, the data now available could fill several volumes. Despite the challenging environment with cold water, strong currents, deep trenches, dangerous reefs, rocky snags and sharp edged shipwrecks, fishing continues close to and on many of these habitats. The implications of this, including the need, and right, for islanders to make a living from the sea as well as other factors such as marine life tourism, sand and gravel exploitation, the search for oil and gas and climate change, remain under discussion.

Fanfare for the Fan Mussel

If you could travel back in time, what period would you choose? One slice of time that would tempt me very much was two weeks in late April and early May in 1971. I was at sea on board a chartered fishing boat, towing dredges in a survey for queen scallops, a small shellfish then (and still) much sought by commercial fishermen. We covered an area from Magilligan in the west to east of Rathlin, and further south.

In five of the 48 dredge hauls completed, large ivory to pale yellow coloured fan-shaped shellfish were caught off the north coast east to Rathlin, some tangled together by fine but very strong threads extruded from the narrow base of the shell. I identified these as fan mussels *Atrina fragilis*, then known as *Pinna fragilis*. They were lifted from shell, sand and small stones substrates in depths from 44 metres (144 ft) to 100 m (330 ft). Some were sizeable, as much as 30 cms long (1 ft) and we must have caught – from memory – at least a dozen, as there were up to three together in four of the five tows, and one mussel in another.

No more were seen alive until a single specimen was found close to Rathlin during a diving survey in 2007. This caused great interest and its precise locality was carefully recorded. Had I realised at the time (1971) how little was known of this mollusc in Irish waters, more attention to its occurrence and biology would have been a worthwhile project.

Found from northern Britain and Ireland south by the Iberian peninsula and into the Mediterranean Sea, the fan mussel is an extraordinary creature, not least because of its fine golden threads of great strength that it spins from a special gland. It uses these to anchor itself amongst the shell, stone and sand sea bed that is its preferred habitat. Long known as a kind of golden silk, these *byssus* threads – to give them their proper name – were called *Pinna Silk* in Italy. During a long history of exploitation (it was also good to eat) these mussels provided threads that were sown into royal garments and made into ladies' gloves and muffs. It is reported that small items are still produced using these golden threads for the tourist trade in Italy. The Rathlin fan mussel site was revisited and carefully searched in 2009 but this apparently last specimen could not be located. Has this amazing shellfish once known as the *silkworm of the sea* now vanished from north Irish waters? It is very vulnerable to damage by fishing gear, such as dredges and trawls, and also to sand and gravel extraction operations. I still feel pangs of guilt that we, engaged in a well meaning fisheries research survey forty years ago, dredged up these fragile and beautiful animals. They were returned to the sea, some chipped yet none seriously harmed, but we had almost certainly disturbed part of their habitat. Thus the fanfare is, sadly, more for their exit than their return.

12. WHIRRING MULTITUDES

Rathlin's Seabirds

Anyone who has visited a large colony of breeding seabirds will tell you of the great comings and goings of thousands of birds, of the clamouring calls, of the pungent smell, indeed, of an initial impression of confusion and disorder. You can experience all these when overlooking Rathlin's sea cliffs and rock stacks in the months from May through to August. There are published accounts of Victorian naturalists who described such sights in terms of 'countless numbers' and 'whirring multitudes', while resident Catherine Gage wrote in 1851 of the Rathlin guillemots that *"their numbers may be compared to those of midges on a fine day."*

Much of the life of a seabird is a mystery to us. True seabirds are oceanic, spending up to eight months roaming the oceans and only coming to land to breed, or if blown ashore by severe storms. There are coastal seabirds, including several types of gulls which visit farmlands and rubbish tips to feed, or lurk in car parks with a cold and hungry eye on our picnic sandwiches and fish and chips.

Rathlin's oceanic and offshore seabirds coming to the island to breed are fulmar petrel, razorbill, guillemot, puffin, kittiwake and Manx shearwater, although it is not certain if the latter still breeds on the island. The more coastal birds nesting here are black guillemot, shag, common gull, herring gull, black-headed gull, lesser black-backed gull and greater black-backed gull.

During four months of each year, Rathlin is a seabird city. By early May most of the oceanic birds are back on the cliffs and rock stacks and the coastal species are already established at their chosen nest sites. Eggs are laid, young are reared and by the end of August the cliffs have fallen silent again and the birds have departed for the open ocean or nearer waters. Some wander the coastal shelf seas, following trawlers to scavenge discarded fish and offal, others find food where they can. There are always seabirds on or close to Rathlin, but spring and summer are the times to see the spectacular gatherings.

How many are there? 'Lots and lots' was the reply when I asked a visiting group of school-children one June day. A number of surveys have been carried out, notably in 1969, 1985, 1999, and 2007. The first two were hampered by lack of experience and shortage of observers. The two more recent censuses were much more comprehensive: all breeding areas were extensively mapped, photographed and the birds counted from land and sea and repeat visits made to ensure as high a degree of accuracy as possible, given the large numbers. For the statistically minded, the results of the 1999 and 2007 counts are given in Appendix 1. Taking in all twelve known breeding species mentioned above, Rathlin supported at least 143,000 breeding seabirds in 1999 and 115,200 in 2007, when numbers were standardised to breeding individuals (some are counted as individuals, others as breeding pairs or at an apparently occupied nest). In both surveys, the most numerous were the guillemot, followed by razorbill, kittiwake, fulmar and puffin, with smaller numbers of black guillemots, shags and five species of gull. The birds showing the greatest decline from 1999 to 2007 in terms of numbers rather than percentages were the auks (guillemot, razorbill, puffin), fulmar and the gulls. Kittiwakes were down a bit but have shown poor breeding success in recent years. Black guillemots have also shown quite a drop in numbers. Manx shearwaters, as stated elsewhere, seem to be approaching extinction as a nesting bird on Rathlin.

Despite declines there remain many birds seeking nesting space around Rathlin's coast, and there has to be some sort of order within the apparent chaos. If you spend a while just watching the birds and where they are you will notice a pattern: the different species occupy the cliffs, ledges, caves, boulder fields and rock stacks in distinct settlements on their tower-block.

In the basements – the caves and crevices and lower rock shelves – shags, small cormorants with a green sheen to their plumage and a tufted crest on the head, build untidy nests of seaweed, often decorated with coloured things like bits of blue, green and orange fishing ropes or a piece of plastic. The larger cormorant does not breed at Rathlin at present, but has done in the past and there has been a large colony nearby at Sheep Island for many years, just west of Rathlin off Ballintoy. Also quite low down on the cliffs are black guillemots, never as numerous as their brown and white cousins the common guillemots, favouring crevices and spaces between or below boulders.

On exposed ledges of the lower and middle cliffs and on high rock stacks, the guillemots cluster together, crammed in masses so tight at times you might wonder if there's room for any more, then another arrives and shuffles its way into the crowd and maybe one or two fly off at the same time. On the flat tops of the high rock stacks, more guillemots squeeze together. The black and white razorbills prefer individual apartments, here a shallow crevice, there a small ledge just big enough for two and will be found at all levels, some close enough to be showered occasionally by sea spray and others near the very tops of the cliffs. They will also cluster – not quite as crowded as guillemots – in boulder fields and find their own spaces amongst the stones.

The white and grey fulmar likes a little distance from its neighbour, choosing a ledge or a grassy space often high up in the penthouse areas. The various gulls build shallow nest-cups of grasses and seaweeds amongst stones or on rocky and vegetated areas around the lower cliff slopes and shores, some choosing inland marshy areas or the edges of a lake, such as black-headed and common gulls. The kittiwake – a small oceanic gull – is found in great colonies on the cliffs and rock stacks, where it jams a nest of grass and mud on to the tiniest of spaces and shouts its name at its neighbours. It's a distinctive bird, white and grey with dark brown legs and feet and a neat beak the colour of a banana. The wing tips are black, as if dipped in ink.

Two of the seabirds nest in burrows, the Manx shearwater and the puffin. The Manx shearwater was once quite numerous but in the past two decades it has declined, possibly due to predation by ferrets which were introduced to Rathlin in 1988. The more accessible colonies now seem deserted and the breeding sites on grassy cliff ledges are perhaps still visited – at present that is uncertain. The shearwaters only come ashore at night and are difficult to survey on these dangerous cliff slopes. The puffins excavate burrows on grassy slopes on and below the cliffs and can be seen at certain times of the day, sitting outside their homes like portly and formally attired members of an exclusive club. Large white gannets pass by Rathlin in lines every day but they do not nest here – many of the birds offshore will be from the great breeding colony at Ailsa Craig off the Ayrshire coast, visible on clear days as a large hump to the east of Rathlin.

Rathlin's vast seabird colonies have become a tourist attraction, and over each season thousands of visitors enjoy the spectacle described above from the seabird viewing area at the West Lighthouse. In the past, however, the seabirds provided a different resource.

Puffin Stew, Anyone?

Before tourism, before supermarkets and on-line shopping, before reliable ferry services and fast rigid inflatable boats (RIBS) and cars and tractors and frozen foods, life on Rathlin was more challenging. Boats were small but heavy and powered by oars or sail and in winter the island could be cut off from the mainland by angry seas for long periods. It was sensible practice to lay in as much food as possible in summer and at harvest to feed family and stock over the winter: grains, milled flours, hay, salted fish and seabirds and their eggs. The seabird cliffs were, so to speak, the local summer supermarket, the shelves stocked with supplies of protein and oils and fats. The trouble was that these were not readily accessible with a shopping trolley. It took skill and daring to bring in such supplies.

Rathlin has long been occupied by humans. Archaeological surveys continue to give us clues to the lives of early inhabitants and recent work, probably published by the time this book is available, has unearthed remains of Manx shearwater, cormorant and gannet from a Bronze Age site in a sea cave on Rathlin. Seabirds and other birds and mammals featured in human diets long ago – examples are remains found at a 9000 years old Mesolithic settlement by the River Bann, near Coleraine, in Whitepark Bay sand dunes from a Neolithic camp (including bones of the great auk which became extinct in the mid nineteenth century) and at a promontory fort at Larrybane near Ballintoy, occupied around 800AD. Recorded history reveals that throughout the nineteenth century to 1945, seabirds and their eggs were exploited for food, and sometimes the eggs for cash, on Rathlin. Tales of these activities survive in the island's folklore (see that section) but the facts are steadily disappearing from memory and the following is based on my own gleanings over the years, talking to islanders, and from the little that has been published by others. There is a wider literature on seabird fowling and egg collecting covering the North Atlantic, from Maritime Canada to Greenland, Iceland, the Faroe Islands, Norway and Britain and Ireland, and further south. In some of these countries, the taking of seabirds and eggs continues, under licence, in places where the tradition remains strong, notably in the Faroes and Iceland and at one remote island off the Hebrides.

Hunting the Foorins

Some Rathlin islanders still refer to the seabirds as *foorins*. This may have roots in Gaelic, but Linda Ballard of the Ulster Folk and Transport Museum reckons the word originated in the term 'ffrens', a rendering of the combined noise of calling birds on the cliffs. It's a good description; listen to a group of razorbills and guillemots saying 'ffffrrrennnsss' (friends?) to each other – maybe you can choose another word to describe the sound. Puffins say 'aarrr' in a guttural tone and kittiwakes shrill their own names while fulmars cackle like mad witches. Manx shearwaters have to be heard to be believed (see Folklore).

In the 19th century and first half of the 20th century, auks (guillemots, razorbills, puffins) flying from the cliffs to the sea were caught by boatmen holding up nets strung between two oars, or simply knocked down with oars. Others were caught by setting *dools* (snares) attached to pegs driven into the lower rocky ledges where the birds often gathered in groups. Climbing down the cliffs on a rope, or up after landing from a boat, were other ways of getting to the seabirds. Manx shearwaters could be taken from their burrows at night, by hand, and the fat young birds within days of leaving the burrow were particularly favoured. The seabirds were plucked (feathers were a useful commodity for stuffing pillows and mattresses or for selling) and skinned and the meaty carcasses were salted in barrels for the winter. Puffins could also be caught in their burrows, but these tunnels tended to be longer than the shearwaters' and curved up at the end (to let water drain away). Both shearwater and puffin can inflict nasty bites. The young puffin, or *puffling* was also popular due to its fatness. The young of puffins and Manx shearwaters are abandoned by the adults prior to fledging (leaving the nest site) and they live on their fat reserves till they get to sea and learn to fend for themselves.

Over Easy for Eggs

The islanders went over the cliffs for eggs as well as birds. Eggs were a bit easier to collect, especially from some of the gulls which nested around the rocky shores or in marshy areas. National food shortages in World War II resulted in sustained egg collecting on the island as the then Ministry of Food bought seabirds' eggs to include in the production of egg powder.

The eggs of gulls, guillemot, razorbill and puffin were collected for food and for sale. Tales of the cragsmen and others who went egging are found in the Folklore section. Guillemot and razorbills and gull eggs could yield up to 90 dozen in a day's collecting. Herring gull and black-headed gull eggs were the most sought after, and the guillemot's egg was a particular favourite. The habit of birds re-laying if the first eggs were taken was exploited by collectors, but the timing was crucial. In a gull's nest, for example, if there was one egg, it was left until there were two laid, then one could be taken. If there were three or four eggs, then they were left, as there was the chance that the clutch was completed and incubation may have started, thus risking getting 'bad' eggs which contained a developing embryo. Egg collectors were proud of their skills and reputations and providing 'bad' eggs for sale was to be avoided if possible. Cliff climbers carried a canvas bag lined with hay to send the harvest up on a rope to a partner on the cliff top, or equally down to a waiting boat. Sometimes a few eggs might be stored under the habitually worn peaked cloth cap. Cragsmen (and women) were both practical and careful, yet there were accidents, and it was a fatality in 1945 that brought these practices to an end.

Visiting Rathlin today you can enjoy the breeding seabirds (but not as a meal) without needing to know just how many there are, just by sitting at a suitable vantage point and watching them come and go, hearing the clamour and perhaps getting a whiff of the guano-splattered ledges so crowded with birds. We should appreciate them in the knowledge that this is one of the best sites (and sights) in Ireland to experience such a wildlife spectacle, and one where research, education and protection measures are active to ensure that our best efforts might help to conserve such wonders.

Ocean Wanderers

Towards the end of summer when the breeding seabirds leave the cliffs of Rathlin, where do they go?

In September there are few guillemots and razorbills on the sea around the island; here and there an adult with a young bird in attendance may be spotted, or a small group of adults. Puffins are very scarce – they just seem to vanish from the coast of the island. Parties of kittiwakes can be found, resting on the water or in feeding flocks, maybe a hundred or so. The fat young fulmars are leaving the breeding sites and adults are scattered, the occasional one or two gliding past. Only the black guillemots – now grey – the gulls and the shags hang about near the island or wander the coastal waters of the area.

Further out to sea on a trawler, on a two week survey in the second half of September 1973, I am scanning the waters between Malin Head, Rathlin and Islay, mainly in the areas known as the Middle Bank and Shamrock Pinnacle, north and north-west of Rathlin. The dark cliffs of the island – empty of birds – shine in the autumn sun and white breakers curl on to the shores.

Fulmars are the most numerous birds in the area, groups of up to 40 milling about, some following trawlers like ours, scavenging for fish guts thrown overboard. Gannets and kittiwakes are frequent. Guillemots and razorbills are few, scattered about in ones and twos. Single puffins are seen here and there, with some small groups of 10 to 12, but mostly they are also well scattered over the sea. Great skuas harass the feeding seabirds and a few Manx shearwaters drift about, with one or two sooty and great shearwaters heading west towards the open Atlantic. If I had expected to find lots of Rathlin's cliff birds enjoying the freedom of the open water after four months being partially land-bound, I would have been disappointed. So, where are they all?

In winter, as in summer, seabirds must locate areas where there is food. It is difficult to say where the Rathlin seabirds go (although some research on this is under way) but there is increasing information on the dispersal, migrations and wintering zones of seabirds that breed around the coasts of western Europe, and it is known that birds from different colonies mix together in wintering areas.

There are three main ways of finding out where the birds go: observations from ships, oil and gas platforms and occasionally from planes specifically used to search at low level; the recoveries of ringed birds and, more recently, the use of 'geolocators', which are small devices fitted to individual birds that, on recovery (you have to re-trap the tagged bird when it returns to the colony) have stored information that shows the bird's geographical locations whilst it was away.

This is a promising line of research, the results are only beginning to appear in scientific journals.

Recoveries of ringed birds show that many guillemots and razorbills spend a while in the Minches off western Scotland while large numbers spread out over the North Sea. Some scatter into the Atlantic. Puffins also winter in the north sea but research using geolocators attached to puffins from a large breeding colony on the Isle of May at the mouth of the Firth of Forth in Scotland suggest that they may be deserting the North Sea for the Atlantic, particularly the waters around the Faroe Islands, an area where there is risk of them being shot by licensed hunters. Observations and ringing indicate that fulmars and kittiwakes disperse widely in the North Atlantic, even to the edge of Greenland's pack ice and further south to the coastal waters and fishing banks off Labrador, Newfoundland and the northern waters of the Eastern United States. On the European side of the ocean, kittiwakes winter as far south as the Bay of Biscay.

The gannets that we see passing by Rathlin in summer generally turn south. The younger birds travel the greatest distances, joining many seabirds off West Africa, where cold water upwells to the surface and large shoals of fish occur, notably sardines. Here the birds follow these shoals, which are also hunted by village fishermen from the coast and huge foreign trawlers and purse-seine vessels. As gannets age – they take five years to reach adult plumage – they winter less far south, for example in the Bay of Biscay off France. In general, many of our seabirds disperse further afield when young and less so as they age.

Guillemots gradually start to winter a little closer to their breeding sites and can be seen paying brief visits to the cliffs in late winter and early spring, from January to April. The Manx shearwater is the greatest of our ocean wanderers. It makes a lengthy loop migration from Britain and Ireland down to the South Atlantic, across to the coastal waters of South America, back up to the eastern side of North America then across the North Atlantic back to European waters and the home breeding colonies.

The three common auks of our breeding cliffs – guillemot, razorbill and puffin – moult their feathers in autumn and winter, and may be flightless for a period. This puts them at risk of pollution and another problem lies in finding adequate food. Moulting is energy expensive. Rathlin's oceanic seabirds face many challenges throughout the year – finding enough food to raise young, surviving predators while on land, coping with a post-breeding moult, scattering across the ocean, susceptible to hunting, winter food shortages, storms, pollution, some night flyers possibly endangered by wind turbines, coping with climate change (still something of an unknown influence in their ecology).

Winter deaths seem to be implicated in recent declines noted at some Western European seabird breeding colonies and it is a complex job to tease apart the various contributing factors. For many years, we have concentrated on protecting breeding sites and monitoring the status of the birds while they are ashore. Now it is essential to take a much wider view, taking in the disciplines of climate study, oceanography, marine ecology, fisheries science and more, and using sophisticated electronic tags on individual birds that help to track their movements and behaviour when away at sea.

When you come to Rathlin to welcome back the seabirds in spring, spare a thought for their amazing life during those eight months of the year when they are out of our sight, but perhaps not out of our minds.

13. SELCHIES AND LEVIATHANS

Seals

Rathlin's seals are popular with visitors, because they are big, easily seen when basking on rocks by the shore near the harbour and sometimes engage in noisy disputes or perform water aerobics accompanied by snorting and bubble-blowing.

Two species occur here, the large Atlantic grey seal, known in folklore as the *selchie*, and the smaller common or harbour seal. Place-names containing the element *–rón–* are clues to the presence, in the past or now, of seals; the Irish for grey seal is *Rón Glas* and for the common seal *Rón Breacach*. Both can be found in mixed groups in Church Bay and Mill Bay and also at Ushet Port near Rue Point. Around the rugged west and north coasts of the island, grey seals are more usual, and they are said to breed deep in remote caves, from which mournful wailings can sometimes be heard as the seals give voice.

Grey seals have their pups in autumn, on Rathlin usually around October and November. The common seals pup in summer, usually June to August. At breeding times, the seals resort to less accessible areas and we should respect their privacy, whether on the breeding grounds or while they lounge ashore, sometimes seeming to pose for photographs.

Seals, like whales and dolphins, are mammals and breathe air. Unlike the whales and dolphins, they need to come to land to rest, give birth, moult their fur coat each year and for safety. I've seen seals come ashore suddenly when a pod of killer whales was passing nearby. Underwater, seals are graceful and can attain considerable bursts of speed when pursuing fish. A grey seal can dive to over 200 metres (over 650 ft) and a common seal to 100 metres (over 300 ft). Seals eat mainly fish, but will also take crabs and other shellfish. The waters around Rathlin contain a good supply of medium to large fish. I have watched a grey seal surface from a forest of kelp with a large ballan wrasse (murran) and chomp it to pieces on the surface as it is dive-bombed by gulls seeking fishy scraps.

Unsurprisingly, there is a close relationship between islanders and seals, while fishermen's interests often conflict with the lives of seals. Today, Rathlin's seals are respected by the islanders and, in addition, both species of seal are protected by law. In the past, seals were part of a resource providing skins and oil, and elsewhere on the north coast, where commercial inshore fishing was active, seals were actively discouraged from raiding nets and occasionally shot. This happens rarely now, especially with the decline is salmon fishing. A rich folklore has developed around seals, especially the grey seals or selchies, and is discussed in the folklore section of this book.

Cetaceans – the Whales, Dolphins and Porpoise

A Traffic of Whales

The rise in popularity of sea-watching for whales and the records of the *Irish Whale and Dolphin Group* (IWDG) have shown that Rathlin has a modest traffic of whales passing through its cool waters. There are places, such as the south-western approaches to Ireland, where more whales are seen (there are more watchers, too) but in the past decade or so Rathlin has produced variety if not large numbers in terms of whales, dolphins and porpoise. Any encounter with a whale is memorable – it does not have to be an ocean giant to impress you.

The Whale That Jumped

If my sub-title is reminiscent of Kipling – think of the *Just So Stories* – it is deliberate, because the whale incident of 15 June 1974, described below, now seems like fiction or a sea poem.

We were afloat in the *Golden Dawn*, an open fishing boat, about 400 metres (about a quarter of a mile) off the north-west cliffs of the island, loitering with the engine idling, waiting for the tide to slacken and release from its suction a float marking a line of deep-water lobster creels. There was a faint westerly air and the sea was calm although we could feel a gentle swell under the boat. Guillemots, razorbills and puffins whizzed past on sorties to and from the cliffs and a blizzard of feeding kittiwakes swept along a tide rip further offshore.

As we scanned the sea surface for the missing buoy, the waters appeared to part and a whale leapt clear. It was almost a slow motion event. The animal seemed to hang in the air, water running off its smooth grey flanks, before it hit the sea with a resounding smack in a belly flop, throwing up spray. It was close enough for us to see a dark eye regarding us and every detail including the bulbous forehead and distinct snout. A small fin was set quite far back on its dorsal surface.

Before we'd quite recovered from our astonishment, the creature leapt again. This time it was even closer, less than fifty metres, and re-entered cleanly, as if embarrassed by its first clumsy display.

The boat was eight metres (26 ft) in length, and we estimated the whale to be a little longer, about nine metres (30 ft). The views were so good that there was no doubt that it was a *northern bottle-nosed whale*, a first record for these waters.

At the second leap, the skipper nosed the boat slightly landwards, as if reading our minds. How close did we want to be to this wild sea creature? How close did it want to be to us? We did not see it again, as it continued its journey north-east along the edge of the great underwater cliffs of Rathlin that plunge steeply to over 200m (more than 650 ft) depth off this part of the island.

I've since been close to larger whales, humpbacks and fins and the like, but there was something about this particular encounter that was special, that has remained sharp in my memory, and no doubt in the memories of all on the boat that summer day. It was so unexpected, the animal so close, the setting sublime: a calm ocean, massive sea cliffs, thousands of sea birds and, almost in our laps, a large, shiny, water-dripping whale. In terms of sea experiences, you don't get much better.

Leviathans and Lesser Whales

So far, sightings of big whales off Rathlin are few. As I write in summer of 2010, an exciting event took place at the West Lighthouse. In July, a number of the RSPB volunteers and lucky visitors enjoying the seabirds witnessed a large whale surface in the sea below, near enough for a photograph to be obtained which led to confirmation of the species as a *humpback whale*, a very rare sight in these waters – indeed, it may be the first authenticated sighting. In 1979, a rare *Cuvier's beaked whale* was stranded on the island's shores. I've watched pods of long-finned *pilot whales* in waters east of Rathlin in the 1970s and these distinctive blunt-headed whales have been sighted recently close to the island; in Newfoundland they are known as 'pot-heads. *Minke whales* pass offshore – probably more regularly than records show. I've seen them off Torr Head, just east of Rathlin, and further out from boats. *Killer whales* also appear now and then, which are classified as dolphins, albeit the largest of this grouping.

Dolphins are fairly regular in summer – *common dolphins* sometimes in sizeable groups, a party of the rarer *Atlantic white-sided dolphins* was seen from one of the ferries in summer 2010 and *porpoises* are quite regular in the sound and elsewhere off the island. I've seen *Risso's dolphins* off Murlough Bay opposite Rathlin and this species occurs from time to time off the Causeway Coast. There is little doubt that more species and numbers will be recorded, whale-watching now being a popular activity and the regular passage of the island's two ferries providing good opportunities to look out for these sea mammals.

PART TWO - FOLKLORE

14. FOLKLORE ON RATHLIN

Folklore is defined as the traditional customs and beliefs of a people preserved by oral tradition. Folklore stories may be attached to a particular place or to groups, whether these are people or animals or other things.

In the period 1960 to 1975, on numerous visits and during stays on Rathlin, I heard ghost stories and tales of strange beings and picked up some fishing lore and superstitions. It was not, however, until working trips to Africa in 1976, 1978 and 1980-82 that I began to appreciate the complexity of beliefs and superstitions and the importance of the spirit world to certain cultures. In Africa, I realised that the spirit world was an everyday presence in village life and it was noticeable how much nature, especially animals, featured in beliefs and stories and how animals were often linked to villagers' ancestors.

When I returned to Ireland, and to Rathlin, it was with a much wider view of human cultures and beliefs, of alternative ways of seeing things. Part of the value of such folktales is how they enrich those of us prepared to take notice.

Rathlin has proved to be a rewarding source of folklore for those few who have cared to investigate. Much has probably been lost with passing generations and we are left with what has been recorded and published and what survives within the remaining oral tradition. Michael J. Murphy of the former Irish Folklore Commission collected folklore on the island in 1953 and 1954 and Linda-May Ballard of the Ulster Folk and Transport Museum recorded stories of fairies and other beings and investigated seal beliefs and gathered some information on seabird hunting in the period 1978-1984. Various books about Rathlin include snippets of folklore and islander Gusty McCurdy has collected some of the most popular legends in a booklet published in 2006. My notebooks contain a number of bits and pieces about fairies, seals, mermaids, other mysterious animals and a good deal of fishing lore and superstitions, as well as tales of intrigue and local adventures. Stories on the island today may reveal modifications while others remain unchanged, but they are being passed on, which is encouraging.

My interest is in linking folklore with nature, to bridge cultural and natural history through stories and beliefs that demonstrate keen observations of nature and different ways of interpreting these.

Having set out my motivation in this rather formal way, let me state that gathering such lore has been, and still is, very enjoyable and rewarding, and in all the years visiting Rathlin I've ended up with a diverse amount of material which, with the help of published work and contact with specialists in this field, has greatly increased my knowledge and enthusiasm for the subject. What follows is based on my fieldwork and the work of others and all sources are cited and acknowledged later.

15. PLACE NAMES

Word Map

The 450 or so place names listed and interpreted by Dónall MacGiolla Easpaig (1989-90) provide a word map of Rathlin, linking places to history, folklore, people, nature and agriculture, plus a few other topics. Few are unique to the island, as a search of Joyce's three volumes on Irish place names will reveal, but notable are the anglicised names of Bruce's Castle, Bruce's Cave and The Axe Factory. Almost all the rest are derived from Irish, an Irish that was not immune to Scottish Gaelic influences.

My breakdown of these names into broad headings linked them to history and human activities in the past, to topographical features, adjectives attached to the names, some associated with nature, others linked to agriculture, and the remainder touching on folklore, proper names including people, sounds (roaring of the sea for example) and a few other odds and ends. There was quite a lot of repetition and cross-referencing in the 450 total of place names analysed.

What makes this exercise interesting is how it reveals that the islanders – no great surprise here – knew their home intimately and how some of the names given to places record long past events. The land and sea are palimpsests of island lore, a multi-layered record of island history. No doubt a closer examination would find even more names, of individual fields for example and even more coastal features, but such knowledge is gradually vanishing.

As a naturalist, I was fascinated to find eagle and wolf mentioned, although the latter is a fanciful connection. Other clues to Rathlin's wildlife were eel, sea bream, seal, pigeon, mice, otter, badger (surprising, as no records exist for the latter two species on the island), cormorant, grey crow and more. Food, other than fish, came under agriculture with mention of rye, barley, pigs, cows (bulls and calves as well), hens, horses and bees. In terms of folklore, there were *gruagaghs* (brown hairy fairies), grey men, hostages, foreigners and good luck (for bad luck stories we must turn to fishing lore).

Amongst the names linked to history and past activities were references to the island's sweat houses, kilns and kelp production from seaweed, burial grounds, silver or money (coin hoard?), mills, castles, graves and so on. At least 22 names of people were recorded, excluding historical and near-legendary folk such as Robert the Bruce, St. Patrick, St. Éinne and Grianán.

There is a richer folklore on Rathlin than recorded in the place names and relatively few listed in the 450 could be linked directly to folk tales or fairy houses and suchlike places, perhaps half a dozen in all. There may, of course, be many more that are unrecorded and remain in the oral tradition, as mentioned in the piece on fairy lore.

Not recorded at all in the list of 450 place-names were sea marks. Fishermen long used reference points visible ashore as alignments to mark particular fishing grounds or dangerous rocks and reefs. Some still do, despite modern navigational technology. On the North Antrim coast, these marks are known as *meiths*. I first heard it used by Dunseverick fishermen, who showed some of the marks back in the early 1970s. It also occurs in Scottish dialects, referring to fishing marks. Meiths are not so much single names as descriptive phrases, such as 'The Baden Rock in the Barn End' or 'The Steucan on the Bridge Gap'.

Cowports and Íneáns

Approaching Rathlin by boat from the west or north one might wonder where to land, such is the rugged nature of the cliffs and rock stacks rising from the sea. For a long time, piers on Rathlin were little more than a thumb stuck into the sea from a hand that gripped the shore where it could. The piers offered little shelter and served as somewhere to load and unload but when it turned rough vessels had to leave or be hauled up the shore to safety. However, having spent many days at sea around Rathlin with island fishermen, and dipped a little into the deep pool of place-names, as well as scrambling down to the sea from land wherever I could find manageable access, it became clear that there were more ports than piers, as well as intriguingly named nooks known as *íneáns*.

Between the Bull and Cow rocks at the extreme west end of the island is Portnaboe, the Port of the Cow. Continue around the coast clockwise till you return to Portnaboe and you find at least 25 places with the word *Port* included and 12 containing the element *Ínéan*. There may be more – it depends on your source of information. Some of these spots seem unlikely landings for a boat or to gain access to the cliff tops, others are more obvious havens. They were not all landing places. Some ports served as a location to bring a small boat close in to cut seaweed for kelp production and get it ashore to be stacked on low stone kelp walls to dry. Others were sites where a boat could be beached or moored a while, as long as the wind was in a safe direction or it was calm. A few had small jetties and served as seasonal harbours. The two main ports were Portandrian, the pier on the north-east side of Church Bay, still in use but eclipsed by the relatively new main harbour opposite. The other, now little used, is Ushet Port near Rue Point, once a place to load and unload grain and other goods, including smuggled items.

Ínéans are grassy routes down to the sea between cliffs. Some provide relatively easy access, others are quite a scramble. The word crops up in western Scotland, on Arran and the Kintyre Peninsula. In the latter, writer Angus Martin calls a favourite spot the 'Eenans', from the Gaelic word 'Ineans' without diacritics. On Kintyre this represents a grassy coastal area bounded by steep rocky slopes in the form of a kind of amphitheatre. This matches a few of the Rathlin ínéans although many here are steep and quite narrow. They are remote and evocative places, giving one a real sense of isolation and spots where I've brewed tea and fried sausages over a driftwood fire. Martin seems to like doing this – the cover of his book *Kintyre – The Hidden Past* shows the author at the Eenans clasping a hot drink by a drift-wood fire with a kettle on the boil. The Ínéans, like other Rathlin place names described above, are descriptive, for examples: *Ínéan na Fideoige* – the nook of the plovers; *Ínéan nabh Fear Liath* – the Ínéan of the nine grey men, a place where nine men were drowned in a shipwreck and later the same number of grey-haired men were reportedly seen walking up this access to the cliff top; *Ínéan na Bó* – the Ínéan of the cow; *Ínéan Riabhaigh* – the Ínéan of the lousewort (a small wildflower).

The names of the little ports are equally illuminating, referring as examples of ancient forts, shipwrecks again, flagstones, fortune or good luck, kids (possibly goat kids) and one or two named after people.

Of the 25 ports and 12 íneans I've looked at on Rathlin, 14 of the former and eight of the latter were on the rugged western arm of the island and the remainder on the lower lying and only part cliff-bound southern arm. Thus the island was well served in terms of access from the sea and cliff top despite its formidable appearance to the mariner and daunting coastal terrain for those wishing to get from high ground to the shore or vice-versa. Many of these remote sites were long known to islanders – still are in many cases – and also served as somewhere to get to a good shore angling location, for catching fish by line from rocks was an important activity in food gathering and is still pursued for sport.

16. FOLKLORE AND NATURE

Those who dismiss folklore as hearsay and romantic nonsense miss an important point. In a past time when people lived closer to nature in order to make a living from land and sea, they kept a keen eye on weather, seasonal changes and the behaviour of wild and domestic animals, often recording in their stories astute observations of nature, interpreting these in different ways.

On Rathlin, stories about seals, seabirds, hares, cats, dogs, horses and other creatures, including the less-classifiable such as mermaids, reveal how islanders in the past related to their home and the sea around it. The following examples of folklore linked to nature and the use of natural resources on Rathlin are set out according to the animals concerned. Some I heard myself, others are gleaned from the literature cited. All of them enrich Rathlin's culture and are a window on the past – one over which we should not pull a blind.

Seals

Basking much of the day on rocks and along the shore, scratching lazily with a flipper and occasionally lifting a smooth, dog-like head to peer at you myopically with rheumy eyes, seals are not difficult to watch on Rathlin. Indeed, they seem curious about humans, and while not relishing close approach when resting ashore, once in the water they will swim quite close to you as you watch from the shore. There is one regular bather in Mill Bay whom I've seen swim unconcerned as the seals splash and snort close to him, while other heads pop up and the dark eyes follow this strange hairless being that dares invade their domain. However, this is an activity not recommended, because seals can be unpredictable and are capable of inflicting a serious bite.

Fishermen, understandably, have close relationships with seals. I choose the word 'relationship' with care, because one of the most widespread – certainly in the North-East Atlantic area – beliefs held by coastal dwellers about seals is that they are the souls of drowned seafarers, even reincarnations of such folk lost tragically at sea.

Relationships are not always good from the fishermen's point of view. Seals have a great appetite for fish and will raid nets and help themselves liberally, maybe taking just a bite from several fish but leaving them useless for market. Commercial salmon fishermen along the coasts generally despise them and in the past, when fixed nets were common along the Antrim shores, raiding seals were occasionally shot. There was never a salmon fishery on Rathlin, and seals here have led a relatively trouble-free life alongside islanders. That's not to say they were never shot at or hunted here, but information on this is sparse and certainly today's numbers suggest seals at Rathlin are thriving.

Seal Stories and Beliefs

Linda Ballard recorded the following statement from an islander referring to the origin of fairies and seals:

"Well, I heard a yarn, it's the time of the rebellion in heaven, and they were cast out, and some fell on the land [and became fairies], and some fell in the sea, and the seal, he's the one that fell in the sea."

A story I've often heard on the island, and one published by Ballard, is that once an islander made ready to shoot a seal when it spoke to him by name and pleaded for mercy, which was granted. One would not be surprised if that islander man never bothered a seal again.

The first tale about seals that I heard on Rathlin – it was almost 50 years past and I forget who told it to me – was that they had a fierce bite and that to protect themselves, those who went into caves after them would stuff their jacket arms with cinders. When the seal bit, it was claimed, it let go on hearing the crunch. It wasn't clear whether my informant was referring to seal hunting on Rathlin or to something he'd heard from elsewhere.

Many seal stories on Rathlin have counterparts in the western isles of Scotland and down the west coast of Ireland. Seal catchers in County Cork wore bags quilted with charcoal on their arms, for the animals released their hold when they bit on crunchy charcoal. A similar story was also told in County Kerry, related by David Thomson in his *The People of the Sea* and I heard a version on Achill Island over forty years ago. In 2008 I picked up a tale in the Sperrin Mountains of County Londonderry, relating to otters – to protect yourself from bites when hunting otters, tie a few sticks around your legs, the cracking of which when bitten led to release.

The Atlantic coast seal stories usually refer to the large grey seal (the *selchie* of Scotland) which is widespread and breeds on remote boulder shores and in caves, its young born in late autumn. On Rathlin both grey and common (= harbour) seals occur, but the grey is the one found on the rugged west and north shores of the island, while the two may be found together on the east and south shores and around Church and Mill Bays near the harbour.

The sight of seals on Rathlin basking on the rocks is interpreted as a sign of settled weather but if they vanish to sea then it is said that a storm is coming. Scientific studies have shown that oceanic seabirds can sense approaching low pressure associated with storms and will fly away from these. Perhaps seals have similar skills. If the cow is on the hill, the weather is set fine, if she's down in the hollow, beware bad weather – a land version of this forecasting. These animals are not predicting the weather, they are reacting to it with senses much sharper than ours; we do the predicting, based on what we see them do.

Ballard has a tale of a man out fishing with a companion and he commented on the mournful wailing of the seals but his friend heard nothing. Later that day the hearer lost his uncle to a heart attack and took the sound of the seals to be a warning, or omen.

The next bit of folklore is about mermaids, but the theme of the story is equally applicable to seals and its core is part of a widespread set of folktales along the western seaboard of Ireland and Scotland.

Mermaids

Half human, half fish, the *mermaid* in sea folklore is a world-wide phenomenon. Fish-men or *mermen* are also recorded in the literature. Peter Anson, in *Fisher Folk-Lore* devotes eight pages to mermaids and mermen – a mermaid was seen in 1911 at Campbeltown just across from Rathlin on the Mull of Kintyre and Anson comments on numerous other reported sightings around Scotland. Not all were pretty females with golden hair and large breasts – some were small, scaly and distinctly ugly.

The Rathlin mermaid story told to me is similar to many published versions. An islander fishing off the shore on the north side spotted a mermaid on a rock and eventually managed to capture her. He'd been told that if you took her tail away, the mermaid could not escape. In need of a wife, he removed this mermaid's tail (as you would a coat) and she lived with him for some time and they had two children. One day when he was off the island, the children found the tail stashed away and showed it to their mother. When their father returned, his wife had gone, returned to the sea. Replace the mermaid with a seal and the tail with the coat of the seal, and this story occurs widely on the Atlantic shores of Ireland and Scotland, and further afield.

Seabirds

Rathlin abounds in seabirds, especially during their breeding season from April to August. They've been coming here for millennia as evidenced by the finding of seabird remains in an island cave midden dating to the Bronze Age. Rathlin's seabirds have entered the island's folklore mainly through the practise of taking them, and their eggs, for food or for sale, which only died out in the 1940s, and the behaviour of seabirds around the island has also been noted as useful indications of the whereabouts of fish shoals and signs of approaching changes in the weather. The belief that some seabirds are souls of fishermen lost at sea is also recorded.

What follows contains information that is part of the island's social history. I've included it all in the folklore section because hunting the birds and their eggs features in many island stories and there has been quite a rise in interest in such past (and present) activities in the North Atlantic in recent years amongst folklore specialists. Several fascinating papers have been published relating to new information collected in Scotland and Ireland.

Cliffs and Birdmen

Before discussing folklore relating to hunting seabirds for food, it is worth noting some facts about seabirds and man in the past. The large nesting colonies did not go un-noticed by visitors to some of them. An example is the seabird breeding assemblage at Flamborough Head in Yorkshire. Despite collecting their eggs, the locals respected the birds - their cries helped guide fishermen home safely in thick fog, and the gulls were seen by farmers to eat insect pests in their fields. However, as the Victorian railway network was extended, men travelled by train to this site, hired boats and went shooting the birds for sport. Kittiwakes, nesting on inaccessible ledges and in great numbers, tend not to fly off or mob predators when they approach, thus they are particularly vulnerable to shooting. This carnage did not go un-noticed, and a number of ornithologists eventually managed to publicise this massacre and in 1869 the *Preservation of Seabirds Act* was passed, the first such bird protection Act of Parliament.

The western and northern cliffs of Rathlin are formidable in their height and ruggedness. At sea level, caves and rocky platforms receive the full force of Atlantic storms and the waves they generate. The western edge of the island has several tall rock stacks rising like castles from the shore and in a few cases out of the sea itself. All this is grand scenery to us but home for four months to seabirds. It was in this challenging terrain that many islanders sought these birds, a resource providing eggs, flesh, feathers and oils. When this activity first began is not on record or in living memory, but there is knowledge amongst present day islanders of seabird fowling and egg collecting on Rathlin in the 19th century and up to the mid 20th century and the above mentioned Bronze Age finds of bird bones suggest the practice goes back a long way.

To stand on the top of a hundred metre cliff and contemplate going down on a rope attached to an iron stake, without any of today's sophisticate rock climbing equipment, is something I can barely imagine. Equally, starting at the base of the cliffs from a rocky shore or a boat bobbing in the swell, is just as daunting to my mind. To the islanders who were 'climmers', that is, cliff-climbers, it was just another day's work. They grew up playing close to fearsome cliffs and many had no fear of heights but certainly had a respect for the dangers. Basalt is a tricky rock to climb, tending to fracture both vertically and horizontally. Heavy rain can loosen cracked parts of cliffs and cause rock falls, and in cold weather, freezing water expands and the ice pushes sections of rock free. The crumbly, weathered parts of basalt cliff faces and rock stacks also add to the hazards for climbers. The denser, harder dolerite,

2.16 Stacknavarlea below the West Lighthouse

2.17 Seabird hunters on Rathlin, circa 1900 - courtesy Tommy McDonald

2.18 Chalk cave near Cooraghy

2.19 Painted Lady butterfly

2.20 Kelp store in Church Bay

2.21 Cooraghy pier

2.22 Underwater life on Rathlin - Photo by Claire Goodwin

2.23 Wild angelica

2.24 Chalk gate pillars

2.25 Belemnite fossil

Stack channel

Wall

Spongosorites G

Duncan's Bo Wall

The Arch   Cave Gully

2.26 Sonar imaging of Rathlin's deep north coast - JIBS

2.27 Feral Goats of Rathlin

2.28 Doon point columnar basalt

2.29 Spot the guillemots!

2.30 The Golden hare of Rathlin - Photo by Tom McDonnell

formed when magma was intruded in places through existing basalts and cooled, is a preferred option for rock climbers, as seen in the popularity of nearby Fair Head as a venue for modern rock climbers. Chalk is also a hazardous climbing rock – full of sharp flints, pitted with holes and weakened areas and equally susceptible to erosion as basalt. The Rathlin cragsmen knew all this, but the lure of birds and eggs was great, and unlike today's rock climbers (kitted out in technical clothing and shoes and with the benefit of specialized ropes and protection devices) the islanders worked in everyday clothing and climbed free or with the aid of home-spun ropes (later manufactured ones). The only other climbing gear employed was the occasional short length of ladder that might be attached seasonally to the base of some cliffs and rock stacks to help gain access to the first ledges.

There is a considerable world-wide literature, some of it in folklore and some in historical and other island accounts, on human exploitation of seabirds and their eggs, down and feather, their skins, fats and oils – indeed any or all parts of the birds, their eggs and their young. The tradition contributed to the extinction of the flightless great auk by the mid 19th century but more sustainable (an arguable point) harvesting of the birds existed on both sides of the Atlantic and some seabird populations are still exploited by cragsmen, notably in the Faroe Islands and Iceland, and at one site in the Outer Hebrides where young gannets are taken for food. In some cases the traditions became deeply embedded in island culture, such as at the St. Kilda island group north-west of the Outer Hebrides, and in particular the now extinct cult of the birdmen of Easter Island in the Pacific. Here, young men competed to collect and return with the first seasonal egg of the sooty tern, having to swim shark-infested waters to and from the terns' nesting stack. These stories are preserved by the Rapa Nui people of Easter Island and in the rock carvings (petroglyphs) near the place of this ancient rite.

Tales From the Cliffs

The main species sought on Rathlin were the auks – puffin, guillemot and razorbill, or 'parrots' as they were known to some. Fulmars did not nest on the island prior to the 1920s so, unlike more northern islands, they did not feature much in fowling or egging. The eggs of gulls and guillemots were popular and in the days when Manx shearwaters nested here in good numbers, in burrows on the slopes and on remote cliff tops, the young of this ocean wanderer were prized for their fatness and flavour.

The stories of Rathlin's 19th century cliff climbers who sought seabirds and their eggs centre on one man, Patrick John Morrison (1838-1919) of Kinramer South, known as 'Paddy the Climber'. His exploits over a long life are documented in numerous sources including the Gage family ledgers, naturalists' publications, books and the island's oral tradition. A few photographs of Paddy survive, notably one by the well known photographer R.J. Welch taken in 1889 and an interesting one published by Alex Morrison, taken about 1901 and showing Paddy with one of Rathlin's female cliff climbers (Rosie McFaul) and three well kitted-out visitors, prepared for an expedition to the cliffs.

A big man, very strong, was how Paddy was usually described. He was famous for his fearlessness and for his knowledge of where, and how, to find birds and their eggs. He was hired to find eggs for collectors and to guide them to the best sites. A man who never married and who, in a story often repeated, sometimes descended and ascended the cliffs by way of a rope attached to a leg of his horse. True or not, this tale seems typical of a man who would take on any challenge of strength or daring.

There were others who pursued this dangerous occupation in the 19th century but their stories are lost to us, save for scraps of tales now part of the island's folk tradition. The exploits of cliff climbers and egg hunters in the first half of the twentieth century are now, as one islander told me, passed on as 'hearsay'; second-hand information about the activities of fathers, uncles, aunts, husbands, mothers and other relatives and friends. This does not lessen in any way the skill and daring of these people, it just makes it a bit more difficult to interpret what took place as men - and a few daring women - dangled and spun on ropes or clambered across slippery rocks and struggled up cliff faces.

To experience what it was like to go after these birds and their eggs, you have to get close to the colonies. Numerous sea trips around the island in small boats in pursuit of lobsters and crabs or to census the birds have given me a feel for what it might have been like to seek, for examples, guillemots and their eggs. Foorins' Cove between Derginan Point and Ruecallan has been known to generations of cliff climbers as a haunt of dense concentrations of breeding guillemots. Approaching by sea – the only access – you hear a hum like swarms of bees, then as you get closer this becomes a louder 'uurrrr-uurrrr-uurrr' as 12,000 or more guillemots discuss your intrusion. To get at the eggs necessitated climbing to the broad ledges where the birds were crowded 10 or more deep in long lines like cans on a supermarket shelf. Care was required not to spook the birds, for a rush of guillemots leaving the cliff ledges could knock you off balance. These are quite big, solid birds that fly fast, and I've felt the whoosh of them passing close over my head when clambering about the lower ledges to get a counting vantage point.

Razorbills prefer to lay their egg amongst boulders or on small ledges or in nooks and crevices in the cliffs, so a colony of razorbills is not as densely packed as one of guillemots. Nevertheless, there are areas below the northern cliffs where razorbills occur in large numbers, sharing the cliffs and boulder fields with guillemots.

Puffins choose burrows to lay in, and this makes them susceptible to trapping either by use of a net across the entrance or by the simple method of reaching in to the burrow or digging it out, processes risking a sharp nip of your fingers from the formidable puffin beak. Another burrow-nester is the Manx shearwater, the young of which were collected a few days prior to leaving the burrows for the sea, as at this stage they were fat and considered very tasty.

Mary Campbell (1951) writes of the social division that existed on the island – still bantered about today – of the islanders from the upper end who were known as *foorins* (meaning 'the birds') - after their habits of climbing the cliffs and eating birds and eggs - and those of the lower end known as *cuddens*, a type of small fish they caught. In the 'old days', it was said, the foorins spoke a purer Irish and had less contact with visitors than the cuddens of the lower end, whose Irish was influenced by their use of English. Whatever the variations between the two parts of the island and their people, this division seems to have been a real one and the cause of occasional disputes.

Alex Morrison (2003) describes how, at the age of 11, he learned cliff climbing from a nephew of Paddy the Climber. He tells of climbing the rock stacks without a rope up to 1945, and how the Ministry of Food bought Rathlin seabird eggs to include in the manufacture of egg powder during World War Two.

Wallace Clark (1995) admits to feeling safe as he went down the cliffs many years ago after shearwater eggs, supported on a rope held by an islander who himself was a climber and is shown in a photograph with a freshly captured young Manx shearwater.

Michael J. Murphy in 1953 and 1954 was told various stories of cliff climbers, including exploits of Paddy the Climber. He heard how the cliffs were divided, like a rundale system, for the collection of seabirds and their eggs, a story previously picked up by geographer and folklorist Estyn Evans but refuted by islanders I spoke to in 2009/10. Perhaps in times of higher human population and during much collecting, the cliffs were formally allocated, but in more recent times (first half of twentieth century) I was told *"they went where they pleased – the only divisions on the shores used to be for collecting the seaweed."*

However, there was a tendency for climbers to work the patch they knew best, often an area of cliffs close to where they resided, and this form of territoriality was respected by other climbers. The division of cliff areas may have existed in the near past but perhaps not as formally as some investigators reported.

Collecting eggs was carried out by women as well as men. One island lady, in her late seventies, told me how she preferred guillemot eggs to gulls' eggs, for *"the gull's a scavenger while the guillemot feeds in the sea."* Their eggs, she said, had pale yolks and were delicious – good also for making bread and for feeding to calves early in the season, to put a shine on their coats. The seagull eggs were sold for cash – five shillings (a shilling now 5p) a dozen for the herring gull eggs and three shillings and sixpence (about 16p) a dozen for the smaller gulls such as the black-headed. *"I paid twenty eight shillings and six pence for a new pair of shoes from the egg money!"*

Those who climbed down the cliffs used two ropes, one for support and one to signal to those holding the rope to tighten up, or give slack, or that the climber was going left or right. Dangerous work, and what put a final seal on an already diminishing tradition of cliff climbing and egg collecting was the death of a young climber in his early twenties in June 1945. He'd gone to the cliffs after rain – a risky thing to do – and had let go of his rope to negotiate a projecting rock which came loose and caused him to fall to his death. *"It put shock waves all around the island"*, I was told.

Kelp

Another hazardous shore activity was the gathering, drying and burning of seaweeds to make kelp (see the earlier chapter on this). Aside from the historical interest of an industry that ran from the 1700s through to the early 1900s, stories from kelp production have entered the island's folklore, and these give a much more vivid picture of the kelp workers' struggles than dry statistics about harvesting and sales.

Three phases of the work all had their risks: cutting the weed at sea and gathering it from the shores, carrying it up cliff paths to the drying areas, and burning it in open kilns. Men, women and children were all involved.

Hamilton interviewed a kelp widow near the Giant's Causeway in 1784, whose husband had fallen from a steep cliff path while endeavouring to carry a heavy load of kelp up to the top. On Rathlin in the autumn of 2010 I was told of a child falling into a kelp kiln during the burning process and after this tragedy that kiln was closed and never used again. It was a hard job getting the kelp dried and burned during the short summer months and all family hands were needed. One pregnant woman came into labour during the work, didn't make it home in time and gave birth successfully on the steep cliff slopes. Two days later she was back at her work at the kiln.

The kelp smoke was believed by some to have disinfectant qualities. The landlord's wife would leave the windows of the Manor House open to let the smoke from the shore fires circulate. In cottages, it was a practice to burn sea rods (dried stems of large brown seaweeds) to let the smoke fumigate the home. Along the Causeway Coast, I was told that some would deliberately breathe in the kelp smoke as it was said to help respiratory problems – smoking that might have been good for your health! In Scotland, there were those who disliked the smoke and said it damaged crops, had a bad effect on cattle and was suspected to be poisonous.

Carrying heavy bundles of wet seaweed on their backs, Rathlin kelp workers were particularly prone to rheumatism, which in Gaelic they called *peeant fuar* or cold pains. A treatment for this was a spell in one of the island's stone-built sweat houses, where fires heated these cell-like structures and up to four adults could squeeze in for a good cleansing sweat. Island girls liked to use the sweat houses to clear their complexion of the ingrained dirt from kelp burning.

My favourite kelp story has circulated on Rathlin for years and has entered the folklore literature. The hot thirsty work led one woman to take a few drinks too many and she was found drunk and incapable by the road. She was taken to a kiln and left nearby while work went ahead. On waking, she asked where she was. *"You've died in drink and gone to hell"* was the answer. She found some money about her person which she offered to her informant. *"Here, you must know the place better than me – get me a drink!"* The burning fires, the black-faced workers, the acrid smoke – it could have been a scene from hell, indeed.

Swans

In autumn, one of the wildest and most haunting of sounds is the trumpeting of *whooper swans* arriving from Iceland. I've heard it echoing down my chimney at night, and rushed out to see ghostly shapes passing over, once memorably silhouetted against a full moon. In daylight, chevrons of swans can be seen over a grey-green stormy sea, beating their way south. Occasionally, some land on Rathlin, and a noisy party on a lake, hooting and honking, may soon move on to the sea loughs such as Foyle and Strangford, or settle on the Antrim and Derry coastal farmlands in barley stubble fields and where potatoes have been lifted, to feed on grain and small tubers.

It is not surprising to find such evocative creatures as swans featuring in folk tales, and the best known Irish story is The Children of Lir. This tale is so widely published I don't intend to regurgitate a full version here, but a summary puts the island of Rathlin and the swans of Lir into context.

Lir, of the ancient race of Irish people called the Tuatha De Danaan, and his wife Niamh had four children, two girls, Fionnuala and Aev and twin boys, Conn and Fiacra. Niamh died not long after the twins were born. Lir remarried, to Niamh's sister Aoife. In due course, Aoife became jealous of Lir's children, and cast a spell on them, They became swans and were condemned to nine hundred years in this form. Three hundred years were to be passed on the Sea of Moyle, which is about Rathlin Island. Gusty McCurdy of Rathlin has published his version of the tale, and has the swans resting at Carrivinally Lough in the *Quarterland of the Swans.*

Eventually, after 900 years, the spell is broken and the children regain human form, elderly and frail. They are baptised into the Christian faith and die. The defunct wind turbines that have dominated the skyline of Rathlin for some time were named after three of the Children of Lir, but had a much shorter life span. There's a proposal for new wind turbines for the island – if they do become reality perhaps they should be given names with a happier history.

The Firebird

That rare scarlet-billed, red-legged jaunty crow, the chough, now sadly reduced to one pair on Rathlin, has an ancient belief attached to it, and a clue lies in the bird's scientific name *Pyrrhocorax pyrrhocorax* which translates as the 'fire raven'.

It was thought, in the early 17th century, that choughs carried fire sticks and started fires. This may have developed when choughs were kept as pets, recorded as early as the sixteenth century. These birds, like their relatives jackdaws and magpies, have a tendency to collect bright and shiny objects. Mark Cocker (2005) surmises that perhaps glowing embers and sticks were lifted – but reminds us that this relates to captive birds and there is no recent evidence of wild birds having such tendencies to fire-raising.

Beware the Hare!

The hare features in folk tales around the world. I heard stories of hares – always the trickster – in African villages that reminded me of reading the Brer Rabbit tales of Joel Harrison based on African-American stories told by plantation workers. The hare has been translated to a rabbit in many versions of folk tales.

In hill farm kitchens around County Antrim, I was advised to watch out for the hare, for it is a shape-shifter, it can take on human form just as humans can take on the form of a hare. There's a story on Rathlin that matches this. The essence of the tale is an account of a boy offered a half-crown reward (about 12p in today's money) to find a hare for hunters out with dogs. He is told by his granny where a hare might be found, under a whin bush. The hunters find the hare, the dogs give chase and it escapes by running into the boy's granny's home. Here the boy finds his granny, out of breath by the fire, and he has his reward and, knowing how she has shape-shifted, praises her for beating the hunters. Murphy writes of a similar story on the island.

There are other tales on Rathlin of hares sucking the milk of cows, of a hare afflicting a man to put a twist in his face and of how the only way to kill a hare with a gun was to fire silver at it. McCurdy (2010) relates a story of the warrior Fin MacCool (not the giant!) bringing a basket of hares to Rathlin to hunt with his favourite hound called Bran.

Mystical Horses and Giant Cats

Humans have mostly held horses in high esteem and in Irish myths and legends they are often associated with heroic figures such as the godess Macha, the warriors Cúchulainn and Fionn mac Cumhail. Nevertheless, tales of a darker nature exist featuring water horses (*aughisky* in Ireland, *each uisge* in Scotland and *cabyll-ushtey* in the Isle of Man). In Ireland they were said to emerge from the sea and if one could be captured and taken from the shore it could become a prized creature to ride, but if brought near the sea it would re-enter the water and devour its rider.

Rathlin islander Gusty McCurdy (2006) records two of the best known horse legends that have circulated for generations on the island. The *Ceannan Dubh* was a black horse of outstanding beauty and had a spear that projected from its chest. Anyone pursued by this terrifying creature was soon overtaken and impaled on the spear. A woman chased by the horse managed to leap a stone wall and her pursuer collided with the stones and the spear was driven through its chest. Rescuers of the terrified woman found the Ceannan Dubh dead by the wall and buried it under a great mound of stones. It can be raised again if a McCurdy woman by descent who is married to a McCurdy man should walk over its grave.

The McCurdy clan have special powers, for Bob Curran writes of *Lig-na-Paiste*, a kind of serpent-monster reputed to live in a cave at nearby Ballintoy on the mainland, which can only be defeated in battle by a McCurdy of close descent within that clan.

The other famed Rathlin horse is a white one, *an Capall Ban*. In brief, a young man arrives on the island after a storm at sea and hears a story from an island woman of a similar arrival many years ago, but this earlier man later left on a mysterious white horse that he summoned from the waves. The young man tells of his home, a mysterious island to the west of Rathlin, and he too eventually leaves, also on a white horse from the sea. There are elements of other folk tales within this story: opposite Rathlin at Kenban Head is a dangerous submerged rock known as *Carrickmannon* or *Carraig Manannán* – the rock of Manannán. Manann is a sea-god – a trickster and another shape-shifter, who rides his horse *Aonbharr* over the waves. The island may be the one that is supposed to appear at times off Rathlin, known as the green or enchanted island.

Many stories surround the cat. In Scotland, the *cait sith*, sometimes green, usually black, was a huge and fierce fairy cat which left a trail of sparks in its wake. In Ireland the man who boasted to his wife about killing the king of the cats was himself attacked and killed by his own household cat.

Below the Rathlin's great northern cliffs, an islander was fishing from the rocks. He gathered up his catch and set off for home, but was followed by a huge black cat. Fearing attack, he threw a fish to the beast, and, followed right to his house, he kept the animal at bay with more fish, throwing the last one to it as he slammed the door behind him. I heard this tale in a slightly more chilling version, where the fisherman sensed he was being followed by something fearful, always just out of sight. Getting home safely, he looked out next morning to find his dog mauled and dead. Sightings of large cats, usually black, are popular stories in the media from time to time, but listen to tales on Rathlin and you'll find such creatures have been around for a long time.

Ghost Stories

Ghostly horses and unearthly cats are as close as I seemed to come to ghosts and nature. There is no shortage of ghostly tales on Rathlin, but they relate mostly to human beings appearing in some sort of spirit form, as apparitions or presences both seen and sensed. Young girls wandering through long abandoned corridors; mysterious lights seen hovering over the landscape; something twitching at your bedclothes; the appearance of the ghost of a young lad on board a fishing boat: these and other unexplained phenomena confirm Rathlin as an island of ghosts and ghost stories. A selection of tales has been collected by Linda Ballard of the Ulster Folk and Transport Museum, and it is to these that I refer readers with an interest in more detail. Included in these stories are encounters with 'The Devil' in various forms, as well as the ghosts of battlefields, and in Rathlin's turbulent history there were many battles.

Time and time again I was told of the area known as Kebble being the most haunted place on Rathlin. In 1999, I has an opportunity to find out if this was so, staying alone for six weeks in the remote Kebble Cottage, the most westerly dwelling on the island with the exception of the now empty lighthouse-keepers' quarters at the West Lighthouse. Kebble, *An Caibal*, was a burying ground, and island friends teased me that I'd be haunted out of the place by ghosts and who-knows-what. Retiring to bed late on the summer solstice, I was awakened by unearthly gurgling and shrieking, seeming to come from the roof. On going outside, I heard more clearly what I'd already guessed was the source of these noises – Manx shearwaters flying low over the cottage, uttering their scary calls. The sound has been described as 'something akin to witches being sick'. Anyone staying at Kebble that night who didn't know their seabirds would indeed have been justified in saying the place was haunted. Perhaps it is - maybe I didn't pay attention to bumps in the night (wind down the chimney?) or else I just wasn't worth haunting.

The Hairy Fairy

It is not my intention to devote much space to fairies here, as they do not slot easily into my theme of folklore and nature and a study of Rathlin fairy lore has been done by Ballard (see references). However, one creature, the *gruagagh* (said 'grooga') crops up in many Rathlin stories. Sometimes referred to as 'the hairy fairy', it is always a male, a half-human half-fairy being, under four feet in height and covered in a coarse reddish-brown hair. The gruagaghs came to the northern part of Ireland from Scotland via Kintyre, which puts Rathlin slap bang on their immigration route. Tales of other fairies exist on Rathlin, but I've selected the gruagagh probably for no other reason than his character appeals to me.

It was in 1972 that the late Dougal Cecil introduced me to stories of the gruagagh over a breakfast of salty bacon and sweet tea in his Rathlin home at 'The Quarters' near the East Lighthouse. A gruagagh, he said, installed himself at the West Lighthouse many years ago and drove the keeper to distraction with clumsy attempts to help with chores. A benign sort of critter was how Dougal described him. You can never pay or reward in any way the gruagagh for his help and if you try he will flee, howling that he's been paid off and can never return. There's a tale on the island that one woman of the house knitted her gruagagh helper a pair of socks and he left in tears, unable to accept even payment in kind. If we accept him as one of the fairy family, then his benevolence towards humans sets him apart from the more malicious and vengeful creatures that inhabit fairy lore. A kindly, bumbling fellow, the gruagagh is always under your feet and is a workaholic, intolerant of laziness and liable to slap you awake in the morning if you linger on in bed. Workers in the fields taking a tea break would find themselves prodded back to their job by this restless creature. Not a bad companion if it were not for his awkwardness – the general knocking over of things, spillages, breakages, and himself forever tripping you up trying to be of service.

Toigh na Gruagach, the 'house of the brownies', another name for gruagaghs, can be found in Cleggan townland in the west of the island. It is a feature made up of two large stones leaning together, evidence that the gruagagh is a hardy chap, requiring few home comforts, as folklore about him records. He's also found in County Donegal and Sligo, and on the Isle of Man he is known as the *Phynnodderee* and in Scotland he is the *Ùruisg*. It is under the name *brownies* that gruagaghs have been tidied up and tamed. Brownies feature in English folk tales, popularised by Juliana Horatia Ewing in her *The Brownies And Other Tales* (1896).Thus domesticated and ever willing to help about the house, it wasn't a huge step for their name, and motives, to be adopted by the junior section of the Girl Guides. A far cry from the all male, unkempt and hygienically challenged gruagaghs that inhabited (or inhabit?) Rathlin.

So there you have it, one of the island's mysteries; a creature rumoured to show itself only to those who believe, as is said of most fairies. After a long hot clamber about the base of the cliffs at Cooraghy this summer (2010) I came back to my haversack to find that the *gruagagh* had drunk all my water and eaten my biscuits (or had I forgotten to fill the bottle and bring the ginger snaps?). If you are walking home from the island pub late at night, hang on to your hat or the mischievous hairy fairy will snatch it away and leave it on an overhanging bramble stem for you to find next morning.

Other Spirits

Spirits of a more tangible nature featured in *Whisky Galore*, the popular book by Compton Mackenzie about the wreck of the *SS Politician* on the isle of Eriskay in the Hebrides in 1941. The islanders 'liberated' a substantial amount of the cargo of cases of whisky and the story was made into a classic film by Ealing Studios in 1947.

The following two stories are more about human nature than nature in the wild.

In 1884, the British barque (a type of sailing ship) *Girvan*, on passage from Glasgow to Melbourne, ran aground on the reef known as the *Clochan Bo* at the west end of Rathlin. After almost a week she slipped off the rocks and sank. The remains are lying in about 20 metres (65 ft) of water in this most exposed position, a wreck that requires a good deal of care and local knowledge to explore by diving.

Amongst her mixed cargo was a consignment of 500 cases of Scotch and Irish whiskies. As in the Eriskay incident of 1941, official guards were assigned to watch the wreck, and on Rathlin the coastguard of the day and the island's landlord carried out this duty. Despite their observance, islanders managed to remove many bottles of Girvan whiskey. This is no tall tale, for that whiskey graced a number of events on the island over the years and I received two bottles in January 1986 to put in a display at the then newly built Giant's Causeway Centre. It was advisable to declare this small booty to local Customs and Excise, which I did, and permission was granted to retain these for display. In the course of declaration, it was suggested by officials that an unknown proportion of the Girvan's whiskey bottles were spoiled by 'the ingress of sea water', as it were. The scientist in me decided to investigate, with help from friends. One bottle was indeed spoiled. The other was a very fine whiskey and slipped down all too quickly. We re-filled the two with cold tea and they remained in the shipwrecks display until the Centre burned down in April 2000. My report to the officials was able to confirm despoliation (without being quantitative) and I like to think this perhaps helped to close the official file on Rathlin's whiskey galore incident.

There is another spirit-ridden Rathlin story, known as 'the ebb-tide whiskey'. In brief, two islanders many years ago were out fishing across the sound near Murlough Bay. They discovered a large wooden cask floating in the strong ebb tide and retrieved it. The contents were a clear spirit of a quality as fine as any good whiskey. Illicit *poitin* distillation was not unknown around Ireland's coastline in those days, and it was likely that such a cask might be anchored offshore for a period if official searches were operating. This spirit was subsequently bottled and safely stashed on the island and, like the Girvan hoard, bottles were produced on and lubricated various occasions. This story was told to me in the autumn of 2010 while I was marooned on a storm-lashed Rathlin, just back from a wet trip to Rue Point, but sadly no ebb-tide whiskey was produced (consumed long before) and I had to warm myself with a more conventional sample of legitimate stuff.

For details of smugglers and smuggling and other adventures, I refer you to Wallace Clark's book and other accounts of Rathlin's colourful history (see the references section.)

Folklore of Plants

It's an old Irish saying: *"gold under furze, silver under rushes, famine under heath."* This can be interpreted as early form of land classification denoting plants as indicators of soil fertility.

The folklore of plants is a huge topic with an extensive literature, much of it centred on plants as medicine with many herbal cures and remedies, and plants that feature in magic, for examples as charms and curses. A limited amount of information from Rathlin has been published: Michael Murphy recorded snatches of plant folklore on Rathlin in the 1950s but even then he seemed to have arrived too late, being told of deceased mothers and sisters who could cure anything but 'now it's all lost'. It was not just wise women who had the knowledge of herbal treatments and magic, but men also. Plants and their extracts were used to cure cuts and sores, heart problems, asthma, corns, colds and coughs and as effective love charms and potions and were all part Rathlin's plant folklore. In 2009, asking about herbalists on the island, I was given names of several experts now sadly deceased. It is, however, a subject worth further exploration.

The practical and economic uses of plants and their medicinal applications extend beyond folklore and there is now a science known as *ethno-botany* which explores the cultural values of plants world-wide. Nevertheless, it is interesting to see how many modern discoveries are linked to knowledge that existed over previous generations.

A few examples of plant folklore recorded on the island include the use of heather as a navigation aid: clumps were taken on board boats in foggy weather and handfuls thrown overboard so that the direction they floated in could be used to ascertain position, using knowledge of tides and currents.

The widespread use throughout Ireland of St. Brigid's crosses made from rushes to ward off evil was common on Rathlin. Practical uses of plants included horse collars woven from straw or flax, ropes twisted from hay and straw, heather and gorse used as kindling for fires, crushed gorse fed to horses and cattle, and even the occasional lobster creel made from gorse stems, although the main plants sought for this purpose were hazel and willows. It is likely that plants (including lichens) were a source of dyes when weaving was a Rathlin occupation.

Rathlin's flora includes most of the key plants that feature in the myths, legends and folklore of Ireland as a whole. These could be used for medicine and magic, but had other practical uses such as for animal fodder, bedding and household applications from sweeping brooms to thatch on the roof. I give one example of a common wild flower on Rathlin that has a long folk history – the feathery-leaved white or mauve flowered yarrow:

A girl should gather nine sprays of yarrow and keep these under her pillow so that she will dream of the man she is to marry.

A portion of yarrow flower placed under or in the nose and causing a nosebleed will indicate that your loved one is faithful and true; no nosebleed, and questions must be asked.

Hang sprigs of yarrow in the house to ward off evil.

Use yarrow as a wound dressing.

As a cure for toothache, coughs and colds.

A good source to the folklore of Irish wild plants is the work of Niall MacCoitir (2006), listed along with some other relevant references at the end of this book.

Fishing Lore & Superstitions

Working on fisheries research for eight years (1968-75) on small boats around the inshore waters on the northern half of Ireland, and later on larger vessels in the Celtic Sea, the Minches and around Newfoundland and Labrador, I've met a wide range of fishermen, learned how to navigate by landmarks, heard many sea tales, and been advised on a host of superstitions and beliefs that should be adhered to, 'just in case'.

Many of the stories and superstitions were widespread within the areas I worked, and a good number existed, and exist, on Rathlin. I begin with two tales from the nearby mainland coast.

The Giant's Eyeglass

Prominent features of the shoreline, seen from the sea, are useful as markers for locating fishing grounds, or simply reminders of where you've set your lobster pots. In the case of the latter, a story from the shores opposite Rathlin, we were lifting creels by a large rock stack set close to an equally jagged promontory east of the Giant's Causeway. Here was once a perfect arch, but a hungry sea had nibbled around the edges for hundreds of years till this erosion caused it to collapse. That's not what happened, I was told by the lobstermen. What happened was that the arch, known to them as the *Giant's Eyeglass,* met its fate in the year the Government brought in, under the new 1940s health scheme, free spectacles for all. Finn MacCool, the giant who built the causeway, had no further need of his eyeglass, and knowing he'd get a new free one from the powers that be, demolished it.

Stueys

It was the same fishermen who told me of how they made dog-skin floats for their long lines, a story also recorded at Rathlin. This one is true because *stueys* or the floats in question were quite common until modern materials took over. Dog-skin suited because it was thin, strong when properly cured and easily inflated. All orifices and legs and neck were either sewn up or plugged with a wooden peg save one leg, which had a wooden spool put in through which the skin could be inflated and then the hole sealed with a wooden pin. When asked where the skins were obtained, my mainland informers said that a local policeman, 'Tail-light Miller' by name (seemingly he had a passion for booking road users with faulty lights) was also a zealous up-keeper of dog licensing laws. Unlicensed dogs were impounded and… well, you can guess the rest. *"Bitches were no use, too many holes to plug,"* I was told, matter of factly. With pressure-resistant plastic floats now widely available, the Antrim coast dogs can relax.

Aligning marks on land to locate fishing areas was a skill all inshore fishermen developed and used until modern direction finders became available. Some Rathlin fishermen still rely on the landmarks. In North Antrim, such marks were known as *meiths*, from Scottish dialect *meeth* or *meethe*, 'to mark a place at sea by the bearings of landmarks' (*The Scots Dialect Dictionary*, 2000). Numerous marks exist around Rathlin and some remain in use today.

Frass Holes

Rathliners fishing from the rocks for *murrans* (wrasse) and other fish would grind up a ground bait to throw into the water to attract fish. Small hollows or holes in the rocks used to mash the bait were known as *frass holes*. Throwing such attractants into the water was known as *frassing*. Cooked limpets chewed until soft, bits of cooked potato, scraps of unused lobster bait, crushed crabs – anything considered suitable was used for frassing. The word is of Gaelic origin, meaning 'plenty' (McCurdy, 2010). Murrans are not the easiest of fish to prepare, nor are they the tastiest. They have sharp spiky fins, tough scales which need to be scrubbed off prior to cooking, the flesh is soft and insipid and the bones are pale green.

Dried and salted, murrans were once a useful winter food. Two island fishermen told me recently, when I criticised their culinary aspects, that they made a great soup. Take your fish, boil it in a muslin bag then squeeze the liquid through and discard the mess remaining. Add onions and carrots and cook a while longer – a potato or two helps thicken the broth. I have as yet not had the will, or maybe not been hungry enough, to test this recipe.

The Jabble of the Ebb

The tides of Rathlin have their names and their reputations, and their stories too. Bounced about in an open fishing boat from Dunseverick, the tide rip between Rue Point and Fair Head was giving us a hard time. *"It's the jabble o' the ebb"* said the skipper, referring to the jagged waves thrown up by the falling tide racing through this sound and meeting a west wind that did nothing to help the situation. This is one of Rathlin's most respected tide races, known as the *slough-na-mara*, which means 'the hollow of the sea' and I'd encountered it before, as mentioned in the first chapter. Other rough tidal rips, marked with little wavy lines on charts and labelled – rather mildly – 'overfalls' are the *Coirevreckan* and the *Torr Ebb*, and further tides are called *The Bush*, *The Doggan* (said 'joggan') and *The Bag*. These operate over a wider area than around Rathlin – I've felt the boat from Dunseverick argue with the Doggan off Bengore Head between Rathlin and the Giant's Causeway.

When a swell arises and crashes in a foam of white against the rocky coast of Rathlin, the fishermen of Dunseverick would look across the sound, leaving their boats firmly tied to the pier, and say *"the shores are up."* When the shores are up, you pay attention.

In 440 AD, Brecain, grandson of Niall of the Nine hostages, warrior King of Ireland, was travelling in his *curragh* (fast seaworthy boats built of light lathes of wood and covered with water-proofed animal skins) along with fifty others when they encountered one of Rathlin's fierce tide rips. All the curraghs and their crews were lost.

17. SUPERSTITION and BELIEFS

Just in Case ...

Superstition, writes fisheries historian Angus Martin, is a sort of self-protective discipline. Fishermen fear bad luck and wish to preserve good luck. Despite many improvements in boat design and fishing gear and a barrage of health and safety information and rules, fishing remains a dangerous occupation. Witness the recent popularity of television programmes about the hazardous exploits of North Sea trawlermen and Alaskan crab fishermen. Poor catches, loss of fishing gear, breakdown of boats, accidents to crew members – such things are often blamed on bad luck, which in turn is identified with breaking some long-standing taboo, and there are plenty of these, although fishermen would probably not use the word taboo, or even admit to superstition – but would keep to old beliefs, 'just in case'; a phrase I heard many times.

Fishing superstitions and beliefs have themselves proved to be a rich trawling ground for folklorists, anthropologists, historians and others. There's an extensive literature – some quoted in the references – but I've kept to what I've picked up on Rathlin and around the Antrim and Down coastal waters, with a few Scottish and North English comparisons.

Minding the Wind

Fishermen discuss the weather at great length, and no more so than when talking about the wind. *"He that considers the wind shall never sow"* said the wise Solomon, but he obviously had the farmer in mind rather than the fisherman. *"Soldiers whistle, sailors sing"* is another old saw. A widespread superstition, not confined to fishermen, is that it's bad luck to whistle on a boat. You might whistle up a bad wind. Wind strength is not the only factor fishermen consider. *"When the wind is south/It blows your bait into a fish's mouth"* wrote Izaak Walton in 1653 in his wonderful book *The Compleat Angler or the Contemplative Man's Recreation*. He classifies the directions of winds further – the west wind is second best for fishing and the east the worst, leaving the north un-named as third. The fishermen of Rathlin never liked an east wind and those of Dunseverick told me it was a bad wind for catching lobsters. Wind strength is traditionally given in *knots*, that is, the speed in nautical miles per hour, a British nautical mile being 2026 yards compared to the 1760 yards of a land mile. The metric equivalents are 1853 metres and 1609 metres (1.8 and 1.6 kilometres, respectively). On Rathlin, however, there is a tale of a different type of knot.

Sailing from Islay across to Rathlin long ago, as many did, a boat's crew was offered a piece of knotted string by a wise woman. The theory was straightforward - to raise a wind for your sails untie the first knot, for a good breeze loosen the second, for a strong blow release the third, and so on. In practice however, you could go too far. A child in the boat discovered the string, and kept on untying the knots. The boat foundered in a gale, and a lucky few survived to learn the lesson of the knotted string. In North Antrim, it is said that pigs can see the wind. The *Seanchas Mor*, an ancient Irish compilation of wisdom and laws, gave colours to the winds:

"From the North the Black Wind/From the South the White/From the East the Crimson/From the West the Grey."

Never Miss the Boat

This was an early lesson. I missed my Irish Sea trawler by a few minutes and was disappointed it didn't turn back for me. A friendly skipper took me out in a sister ship that was to fish in the same area. The two boats heaved to in a bouncy sea and someone shouted 'jump!' I just made it on to the pitching deck of my intended boat. *"Never again!"* I said. *"Aye, too right, laddie; never miss the boat, it's very bad luck to turn back once you've sailed."*

It was the same on Rathlin – be on time, don't force the decision on the crew to come back for you, chances were that they would not turn ashore. In terms of turning, it's considered bad luck to swing around against the sun; always where possible turn the boat with the sun.

Not a Good Idea...

When I once suggested bringing a female work colleague – a marine biologist - out on a trawler from a County Down fishing harbour, the first question was *"has she red hair?"* I admitted that her hair was *"sort of auburn."*

"Not a good idea," came the response, which really meant 'no way!'

A red-haired woman anywhere near a fishing boat or fishing gear is very bad luck, a widespread belief amongst sea fishermen. I did eventually get my colleague on board a trawler, and that day they landed a very good catch of prawns, but the rest of the fleet remained unimpressed. Red hair in general seemed unpopular, particularly concerning a boat's maiden voyage. Before my hair and beard turned white, a strong red tinge prevailed and I was once refused access to a boat that had just been launched. Clergymen are equally resented near or on a fishing boat indeed it is often forbidden to mention them, or anything to do with the church, the manse and suchlike.

Rathlin has always been a dangerous place to fish, and even with today's much improved harbour the size of the few island fishing boats is small, a feature of most County Antrim small ports and harbours.

There seems to be more 'don'ts' than things that are okay. Don't turn back home if you forget something, don't go fishing if you meet certain women or a clergyman on your way to the boat, don't mention pigs, rabbits or hares or salmon (unless you are a salmon fisherman) – indeed, don't talk about foxes, dogs, curlews, cats, in fact, most quadrupeds, depending on what parts of the coasts and seas around Britain and Ireland you fish. Why pigs, or any of these animals?

It may have something to do with appeasing the sea. You fish in the sea's domain, so keep land talk to a minimum. Green is commonly believed to be an unlucky colour at sea – is it the green of the land that's in question? More negatives – don't launch the boat bow first or she may never return, don't 'bad mouth' the fish or they will desert you, similarly eat your fish from head to tail or the fish will swim away from you, don't carry your fishing boots with toes turned towards the ground or you'll drown before nightfall, don't let your wife do any washing on the day you go fishing or you'll be washed overboard, and never ask a fisherman if he's going fishing that day (I've run out of ambiguous answers to that one).

So what's ok? A boot or a hot coal thrown after you as you leave the house for the harbour is lucky. Geese flying north, that's a good sign. Seeing swallows or porpoises, that's ok. The call of the cuckoo is a lucky sound, unless you're from south-west Scotland where it's a bad omen, unless you've just eaten something.

Not all of the above apply on Rathlin, but many are known there and versions of these were (and are) adhered to, again 'just in case...'

There's an account in Mary Campbell's *Sea Wrack* of a party leaving Rathlin by boat, which includes the minister, some pigs for market and several women. That sounds like a particularly unlucky group, but the author makes no mention of any superstitions and, as the boat was not setting off to fish but employed as a ferry, it must have been alright. Nevertheless, the boat in question was kept from returning to the island for several days by storms...

The custom of avoiding using certain words and replacing them with oblique references was widespread and is still practised. Captain Cook encountered the word *taboo* or *tabu* in the Sandwich Islands in 1784, when islanders, not wishing to offend, asked if anything they might discuss or otherwise consider was *tabu* to their visitors. Alexander Fenton in his study of the sea vocabulary of fishermen in the northern isles of Scotland (2008), found in the sea language of Shetland up to 559 taboo words with a high proportion based on Norse; the list covered land animals, domestic fowl, sea creatures, fish, a wife or women, and much to do with ministers and the church, fire and tongs, natural phenomena, boats and fishing. Many of the words had been gathered in the period 1893-1932.

Peter Anson, author of numerous books on fishing and fishing lore, wrote (1965) that after 40 years of investigating fishing communities he'd instinctively absorbed many of the superstitions. Anson researched a wide area, from Scotland south to Brittany and Spain. He found that there were unlucky names, that is, certain families and individuals having bad luck associated with them; he described how a fisherman's journey from home to the harbour was fraught with risks – he feared meeting any of the unlucky people, anyone with red hair or flat feet, a minister of the church, dogs, hares, any drowned animal washed ashore and it was not worth going to sea if a woman walked on the fishing lines or touched any fishing gear. Once at sea, there were all the taboo words to be avoided. If a rat was encountered on board its blood must be spilled, a cat on the boat was considered unlucky (luckily for the rats!) and a few twigs of the rowan tree kept the fairies' influences at bay.

Alec Gill (1993), investigating folk lore amongst the fishing community of Hull in England, found many similar beliefs and superstitions. He looked into the pig taboo in some detail and found pig associations to be ancient – in general, pagans praised the animal, Christians either feared it or were disgusted by pigs and their behaviour.

I am not overtly superstitious but during the years at sea I respected beliefs and never used the taboo words, I eat my fish head to tail and my luck as an angler has remained good, and, not being a sailing man, I wonder what I did wrong because the only yacht I ever went to sea on sank within yards of its berth – was it my green sweater? Who knows?

What's It All About?

In terms of folklore in general and superstitions in particular, one quote is worthy of noting, a comment by the philosopher Vico (1725) quoted in *The Encyclopedia of Religion*:

> *"Uniform ideas originating among entire peoples unknown to each other must have a common ground of truth."*

In fishing communities it might now be difficult to trace the origins of common beliefs and superstitions. Many of the folk tales described above from Rathlin have parallels along the Atlantic seaboard from Norway to Spain. Similarly, superstitions have travelled, and across the Atlantic in Newfoundland I found a wide range of beliefs common to those in Ireland. Newfoundlanders have a word for the occasions when two ships meet at sea and come together so the crews can exchange news and gossip. This is called having a good 'gam'. Perhaps many folk stories and beliefs travelled in such a way. Fishermen keep in touch at sea – nowadays by radio and mobile phones – and swop stories when socialising ashore. Thus it is not surprising to find common threads throughout the whole gamut of superstitions and beliefs. Other dangerous occupations are prone to superstitious 'just in case...' beliefs, such as mining and mountaineering.

In conclusion, have I been true to my aim of finding in Rathlin's folklore links with nature? I believe so, up to a point. It is almost inevitable that one strays into the domains of myth and legend, which are well populated with birds and beasts, while other familiar animals and their behaviours are part of folklore.

Mystical creatures such as mermaids, variations of the gruagagh, seal beliefs, seabird stories, tales of huge cats, terrifying dogs, legendary horses, shape-shifters such as hares and humans becoming birds – none are unique to Rathlin and some are world-wide in their distribution and variations.

What I find encouraging is how Rathlin's stories have survived, some perhaps modified but with the core elements intact, and how much they demonstrate an affinity with the natural world too many of us are losing or have lost. Take time to sit and watch the seals in Mill Bay, hear them wail and snort and spit and scratch, look into those tear-washed eyes that stare back at you and ask yourself 'who is the more curious?' That's how stories might begin.

PART 3 - THEN AND NOW

18. STRANGE BEHAVIOURS

Naturalists on Rathlin

Those of us who chip at rocks with hammers, scrabble about on hands and knees to identify difficult small plants, chase butterflies with nets, erect night lights to trap moths, peer through binoculars at birds and engage in other apparently strange behaviours sometimes attract the attention of local people who are either fascinated by such activities or are convinced that we are crazy. This has always happened to fieldworkers, from anthropologists to zoologists. Writer and naturalist David Cabot described how the eminent Irish naturalist Robert Lloyd Praeger (1865-1953) was leading an excursion in the countryside when he overheard two locals discussing their activities:

"Where d'you think they've come from?"

"Och, they're from the asylum. That one there [pointing at Praeger] is their keeper."

Today, even with a wider awareness of the environment and environmental work, and the range of nature programmes on television, non-naturalists can still misinterpret the work of innocents such as myself. Trying to count seabirds, lying on a cliff top straining my eyes through binoculars, I've been asked:

"Seen any pirates?"

"Are you a coastguard?"

"Is that an oil tanker offshore?"

A colleague, doing similar work at the Cliffs of Moher in County Clare some years ago, allowed a lady visitor to look through his telescope at puffins.

"Gee, aren't they cute! Can I buy one?"

Another interruption to his counting came, and this time he let the visitor see the masses of guillemots clustered on the cliff ledges.

"Wow! There's millions. It must cost you a fortune to feed 'em all."

Despite interruptions, naturalists persevere. What follows draws on parts of earlier chapters as well as additional research.

Geology and archaeology can throw light on a natural history that greatly pre-dates written history, but it is in the latter that we find more recent descriptions of Rathlin's flora and fauna. The recorded natural history of Rathlin covers about 225 years, from 1784 to now (2010) and will no doubt continue. Birds have received the most attention, which is not surprising given the island's strategic position for receiving migrants and its good diversity of birdlife overall.

The Reverend Doctor William Hamilton, a keen naturalist and an amateur geologist of considerable skill, visited Rathlin in July 1784 and described his findings in a letter, which was just one of a number he collated as *Letters Concerning The Northern Coast Of The County Of Antrim Containing Such Circumstances As Applies Worthy Of The Notice Respecting The Antiquities, Manners And Customs Of That Country Together With The Natural History Of The Basaltes, And Its Attendant Fossils, In The Northern Counties Of Ireland.* First published in 1786, my copy is dated 1790 and contains a hand-written note on the fly leaf which says: '*the author was way laid by a party of defenders and put to death in 1796.*' Hamilton was also a magistrate in his home area of north Donegal, prior to the 1798 rebellion. His account of his Rathlin visit has been referred to in several chapters in this book and needs no further elaboration here.

A decade later Belfast's John Templeton discovered sea kale – a plant now thought to be extinct in County Antrim – growing in Mr Gage's (the landlord) garden, transplanted from the wild. Templeton (1766-1825) was one of Ireland's leading early naturalists and his initials appear after many County Antrim botanical records, some from Rathlin. The Victorian period – 1837-1901 – was a time of exploration and great energy. Naturalists and natural history societies flourished. The British Empire was huge and intrepid travelling collectors of plants, bugs, birds and other flora and fauna sent a stream of specimens back to museums, botanical gardens and private sponsors. In 1821 the *Belfast Natural History Society* was formed, becoming in 1842 the *Belfast Natural History and Philosophical Society* under which name it is still going strong, promoting knowledge of the arts and sciences. The *Belfast Naturalists' Field Club*, founded in 1863, also still thriving, numbered amongst its members field workers who would contribute much to the geology, flora and fauna of Ulster. Rathlin received its fair share of attention, and to travel there and find accommodation on the island at these times did require a degree of 'intrepidness'.

A vivid account of Rathlin in the 1830s was published by Dr Drummond Marshall in 1837. He was a medical doctor and his presence on the island (he first visited in June 1834) was welcomed by a population of whom the Reverend Hamilton had noted in 1784:

> *"the chief desideratum of the islanders is a physician, the want of whom they seem to consider as their great misfortune…"*

Little escaped Marshall's observant eyes and his 1837 paper is much quoted as an early source of information on Rathlin, not only about its flora and fauna but also the social conditions, the landscape and the use of natural resources by an island population then numbering just over 1000 people. He acknowledges the Gage family, the island's landlords from 1746, for providing him with information.

The Reverend John Gage purchased a long lease of Rathlin from the Fifth Earl of Antrim in 1746. His eldest son Robert constructed the Manor House in the 1760s and the Gage family occupied this through several generations until the property was sold in 1975. It is now in the care of the National Trust. The Gages took a considerable interest in Rathlin's natural history. Catherine Gage, wife of Robert Gage the second (died 1862) wrote a detailed history of the island which she completed in 1851 (five handwritten copies for the family). This contains a considerable amount about the flora and fauna, including lists of plants, fishes, mammals and birds. Catherine died in 1852 and her book was eventually published in 1995. There's an account in Mary Campbell's (her mother was a Gage) reminiscences of Rathlin life (published 1951) of Robert Gage the third (died 1891) questioning his *ghillie* (shooting and fishing helper) about a rare northern falcon they had seen earlier. The ghillie managed to shoot it for him and Campbell writes how Robert's sister, another Catherine (died 1892), would make a painting of it for the 'Rathlin Bird Book'. Shooting was both a sport and a way of obtaining specimens, mainly of birds. In this way, there was little doubt about identification. Catherine Gage the artist produced 165 studies of the birds in watercolour over ink, most from the island and perhaps some from elsewhere in County Antrim. The proposed bird book never made it to publication but the folio of Catherine Gage's paintings came up for sale in October 2010 at an Irish auction, fetching 13,500 Euros. Robert Connolly Gage – he of the falcon incident above - compiled a list of the birds of Rathlin, published in Dublin in 1861. The Gage family retain some land and a house on Rathlin and are regular visitors.

Beginning with Marshall's work, the Victorian enthusiasm for collecting and classifying and listing flora and fauna continued at Rathlin. Between 1851 and 1902 naturalists visited the island to record geology, marine molluscs, land molluscs, beetles, foraminifera (tiny marine creatures that make up the ooze that becomes chalk), polyzoa (small marine communal animals) and especially botany and birds. In the latter two areas of interest, notables were Robert Lloyd Praeger who listed the island's birds and plants, and the botanist Samuel Alexander Stewart, who carried out the first detailed survey of Rathlin's flora. Another regular visitor at this time was Robert Patterson, who published detailed list of the island's birds in 1892. Rathlin's rocks were thoroughly surveyed by R.G. Symes and A. McHenry over the years 1883-1885 for their detailed geological memoir (published 1888) of the Ballycastle area.

They were a hardy lot, these tweed-clad and nail-booted naturalists. Praeger, a solidly built man over six feet tall, was a phenomenal walker – during five years of weekend fieldwork he covered 5000 miles on foot to complete his botanical survey of Ireland (published in 1901). There are photographs of him on Rathlin in 1889, wearing his trade-mark deerstalker hat, chatting to Paddy the climber at his cottage and scrambling up the base of Stacnacally. His old friend and teacher, botanist and geologist S.A. Stewart, lantern-jawed and shaggy with sideburns, must have cut a notable figure as he scoured Rathlin's humps and hollows for plants.

By 1900, several key books on Irish natural history had been published. William Thompson's *Natural History of Ireland* came out in four volumes in the years 1849, 1850, 1851 and 1856, the latter four years after his untimely death in 1852 at the age of 47. R.M. Barrington organised a detailed survey of the migrations of birds at Irish lighthouses and light-ships in the 1880s and 1890s which he published in a large, privately produced book in 1900. In the same year R.J. Ussher and R. Warren brought out *The Birds of Ireland*, another detailed study. In all of these, diligent searching will produce many Rathlin records, mostly of birds.

This flush of natural history activities faded somewhat in the years up to and including the First World War. In 1913, two lady ornithologists, Mary Best and Maud Haviland, spent September and October on Rathlin, studying bird migration and 'procuring' many specimens. In 1915, R.F. Sharff compiled a list of Rathlin bird names in Irish. After the war, J.A.S. Stendall discovered the fulmar petrel breeding on the island in 1922, there was a study of mosses in 1924, the Belfast Naturalists' Field Club made useful excursions to the island (1924 and 1925) and in the 1930s the Rankin brothers visited Rathlin to survey moths and birds. Two naturalists who popularised their topics by writing, broadcasting and film-making stand out at these times – C. Douglas Deane, 'Jimmy' to those who knew him, was coming to Rathlin from the 1930s and adding steadily to its list of birds while Lisburn-based teacher Arnold Benington first visited in 1922 and led expeditions there in the 1940s and 1950s to study the natural history.

The 1939-45 Second World War interrupted this flow of Rathlin studies, although in 1940 the noted Belfast born ornithologist and folklorist Reverend Edward A. Armstrong published his delightful account of his younger years as a naturalist in Ulster in *Birds Of The Grey Wind*. Two chapters are devoted to Rathlin, with many details of the birds and the accounts of the author's hair-raising escapades climbing the great rock stacks.

A study of the igneous (volcanic) rocks was made in 1951 and various reports and published papers on the birds by naturalists following in the footsteps of Deane and Benington were written in this decade.

The Rathlin Bird Observatory went beyond listings in 1960 and 1961, carrying out migration watches and ringing birds to help trace their movements. I carried out several seabird counts in the 1960s, and further bird studies throughout the 1970s. In 1969 the first attempt was made to census all the island's breeding seabirds as part of a nation-wide survey known as *Operation Seafarer*. A second, revised edition of the Ballycastle and district geological memoir of 1888 came out in 1966, providing a wealth of detail on Rathlin's chalk and basalts.

An up-dated list of the island's birds was produced by C.D. Deane in 1970. In the same year, the then Ministry of Agriculture moved its Fisheries Research Laboratory from Belfast to Coleraine and, as a member of the staff, I carried out, over the years 1970-1975, surveys of lobsters, edible crabs, queen scallops and marine fishes (and studied seabirds at sea and noted various whales) in the north coast area, many of which included Rathlin's coastal waters. With the establishment of the New University of Ulster at Coleraine in 1968 (now the University of Ulster), scientific staff and post-graduate students took some interest in Rathlin - a stranded Cuvier's beaked whale was examined there in 1979 and a study of Rathlin's freshwaters, mainly of tiny diatoms, was published in 1982. The university has since expanded and diversified and continues to carry out work on Rathlin, notably in maritime archaeology. In 1985 another detailed seabird census was made and also in the 1980s, the first surveys of marine life around the Island were carried out; the shores – the littoral zone – were explored and also the sub-littoral zone or underwater environment close to the island was thoroughly examined by sub-aqua divers from the Ulster Museum. Their two surveys were part of wider work covering all of the Northern Ireland coastline and inshore waters.

The *Royal Society for the Protection of Birds* (RSPB) became involved with Rathlin in 1975 and thereafter. Large areas of the northern cliffs were purchased to help protect breeding seabirds and summer wardens were engaged to monitor birdlife. Gradually other conservation organisations became land owners and land managers on the island, first the *Northern Ireland Environment Agency* (NIEA) who acquired the western townland of Kebble with its important seabird breeding cliffs and rock stacks (some of the latter remain as Crown Estate property) then, in 1996, the *National Trust* (NT) took an interest in the island's built and natural heritage and now owns the Manor House, the kelp store and Ballyconagan townland on the north-east part of the island. Various surveys have been carried out by staff and contracted biologists from these three organisations on Rathlin, as well as by botanists from the *Department of Agriculture and Rural Development* (DARD).

Further all-island seabird censuses were completed in 1999 and 2007 and the past decade has seen an expansion of research in Rathlin's underwater environment, with sophisticated sonar mapping of the seabed and detailed surveys of underwater plant and animal life, resulting in many new finds, including several species of sponges new to science.

The RSPB has added to its land ownership on the island and for many years has operated a popular seasonal seabird watching programme for the public, based at the platform of the West Lighthouse. Tens of thousands of adults and children have enjoyed the spring and summer spectacle of cliff and stack nesting seabirds each year. In the 2010 season, almost 17,000 visitors attended.

A range of international, national and regional conservation designations now envelops Rathlin and help to protect some of its most sensitive and important landscape and habitats and their flora and fauna. The built environment has not been ignored, with several of the historic buildings and monuments and other historic sites (including those in conservation bodies' ownership) having received protective listings and a degree of protection over many years.

A PhD has been completed on the island's ferret population and another, studying the seabirds, is well under way. The latter was prompted by the decline in numbers shown by the 2007 census, and is considering, amongst other things, food supply, feeding areas and possible climatic effects. Specialists in various fields of natural history as well as archaeology continue to visit the island, while many more amateur naturalists and volunteers come to enjoy its wildlife and help with various projects, at the same time experiencing a bit of the island life that is so special on Rathlin.

This brief review has omitted and no doubt overlooked other natural history work on the island and for that I apologise to those workers whose published studies are not mentioned here. These all add to our knowledge of the biodiversity of Rathlin and its adjacent marine life and a detailed bibliography of all to do with the island will be forthcoming soon.

19. ALL CHANGE

Rathlin and Tourism

In 1960, when I first went to Rathlin, there were few visitors and those were mostly naturalists, yachtsmen, lighthouse-keepers going on or off duty, largely people with special interests. The Gage family still owned the Manor House, the island boats were small open vessels and there was the Ballycastle-Rathlin mail carrier, also licensed to ferry a few passengers. It was no larger than the island boats. Conservation was not in anybody's vocabulary then; it wasn't until 1975 that it came to the island in the form of the RSPB, as described above. The corncrake and the chough were present in fair numbers and no-one had, as yet, attempted to census the hordes of seabirds.

Tractors were the main transport on the island. There were a few small cars, ferried across one at a time, precariously balanced on planks set across a boat. Cattle made the same journey back and forth, hog-tied and lying on beds of straw. All goods came and went the same way, except for the occasional emergency supplies brought in by helicopter, also used for evacuation of seriously ill patients.

Now, if you live close to the island's harbour, there are ferries at the bottom of your garden. It's 2010 and I'm writing this sitting in warm sun, perched on a large block of chalk that is part of the foreshore in Church Bay. It is mid-June and brown eider ducks are clucking and fussing around broods of tiny downy ducklings, bobbing in the gentle waves that are washing insects out of a bank of rotting seaweed that is half in the sea and half ashore. The two island ferries are busy departing and arriving, laden with day visitors and in the harbour three cruising yachts are moored while their weather-beaten crews sip beers and swap mariners' tales up at the pub. Several speedboats have come and gone in the course of the morning, one I recognise as an islander's, the others nipping across from the Antrim coast harbours this calm day. Small groups of folk with haversacks and sticks pass by me, setting out on walks, others pile into the 'Puffin Bus' to be bumped slowly to the West Lighthouse to marvel at the great seabird colonies and to hope that they'll see puffins (they will). Cyclists whizz about, some on hired bikes labelled with the island hostel's name. The boathouse museum and information centre is busy, the souvenir shop is trading, the grocery is open and there's a queue at the fish-n-chip outlet. In Mill Bay, about thirty seals are lounging, some with heads up watching camera-clicking tourists and no doubt hoping the photographers won't get too close and put them off their beloved basking rocks. The pub's beer now arrives in a large lorry on the vehicle ferry. This vessel currently has restrictions on taking visitors' private cars to and from Rathlin. Many islanders have at least two cars per head, an old jalopy for use on the island and a more presentable model for trips to the mainland. Numerous households are connected to the internet. An island lobster boat is far out in the channel and I can just see through my binoculars two figures bent over lobster and crab creels on the deck. Every islander is working today, making a living at the start of the peak season.

This is 21st century Rathlin, unimaginable fifty years ago. It's good to see all this vibrancy, but does it come at a cost? How does a small place with a lot of private land – much of it under agriculture – cope with this rising tide of tourism? One needs to be very careful about the answers, especially when not an island resident. I've spoken to friends and acquaintances all over the island, and opinions vary. I cannot interview the seals and the seabirds; nevertheless, I will try and speak for them.

Eco-Tourism

What is this? Put simply, it is common sense applied to visiting places that are unspoilt or relatively so, that have a rich natural heritage of scenery, indigenous people and wildlife, and it is what it says, tourism with a special focus on the ecology – human and wildlife. It also helps if the tourism adds to the economy of the island and the money is not filtered off elsewhere. There's a saying 'leave nothing but footprints, take away nothing but memories.' I'd suggest try to minimise the footprints, the memories are up to you.

Various plans and strategies have been carried out relevant to Rathlin, including a *Rathlin Island Community Strategy* 2008-2013 and a sustainable tourism plan completed in 2005 that looks ahead to 2015. The latter contains a useful collation of information on the natural heritage of Rathlin and considers important matter such as the various carrying capacities the island might cope with – physical, social and ecological. In other words, how many visitors can be present on the island before the places begins to lose what most value it for – its peace and quiet and its wonderful wildlife? There are various island organisations that consider the points brought out in plans and strategies already existing, and are also driving forward their own ideas.

I've chosen to put forward my own views, based on a long relationship with Rathlin's natural environment and many years' experience trying to help manage tourism and nature and landscape conservation on the busy Causeway Coast.

The 2005 survey found that visitors most appreciated the peace and quiet, the wildlife or nature in general and liked to feel welcome. The infrastructure to meet all these desires is not yet fully in place, but it is being tackled with enthusiasm and needs funding and other help. There is no doubt in my mind that Rathlin islanders and the island itself are already feeling the pressure of rising numbers of day visitors, some welcoming these and others being concerned about trespass, public safety and loss of privacy.

The seabird colonies visible from the West Lighthouse platform, a viewpoint operated seasonally by the RSPB, attract a high proportion of spring and summer visitors to the island. This resource is well managed, with the *Puffin Bus* and the *Bird Bus* meeting the ferries each day and transporting visitors the 8 kms (5 miles) to the reception point at the RSPB's Seabird Centre at Kebble, perched above the cliffs with a view to some of the rock stacks where large numbers of the birds breed. You then make your way down steps to the west lighthouse viewing platform, where more information is laid out and volunteers with binoculars and telescopes provide commentaries on the scene.

It is indeed an impressive sight, even with the decline in seabird numbers that has taken place in recent years. Large numbers of guillemots, razorbills and kittiwakes come and go from the cliffs and stacks, and there is a puffin colony on the lower slopes. Cackling fulmars occupy cliff sites close to the platform, ravens are often present (egg thieves) and you might even catch a glimpse of a peregrine falcon and other scarce species. The peak period for seabird activity here is from mid-May to mid-July.

Over 10,000 people visit this site each season, between April and August. In the 2010 season almost 17,000 visitors were logged. July and August tend to be the peak months, although many of the birds are leaving at this time, especially in August.

This spectacle provides employment for islanders and temporary residents, including bus drivers and RSPB staff, and many volunteers - some from far-away places - gain useful experiences and an appreciation of Rathlin. The site is also a recruiting point and promotional opportunity for the RSPB and its work, as well as being valuable for education and research .

If there is any disturbance to the birds – and I have seen none because the site is well supervised – then you only have to consider that what you see here is only a moderate proportion of the total seabird breeding population on the island. As far as eco-tourism goes, this is a good example and possibly the only downsides are the poor quality of the last half mile or so of road that involves much low gear driving and the diesel fuel buses that are ageing and probably in need of a greener replacement.

It's a different matter, however, if you want to approach these birds by sea, perhaps on a fast RIB (rigid inflatable boat) around the base of the cliffs. Here, hundreds if not thousands of birds are on the water close to the breeding ledges and need peace to wash and preen and inter-act. It's a messy place, the breeding ledge or burrow, and parasites such as mites and ticks build up in the plumage; a good splashy bath and some vigorous preening helps. The guillemots in particular, crowded close together on ledges, can be spooked easily, and a mass flight from these can result in eggs knocked into the sea. Seabird viewing trips in boats are becoming popular and, as with whale watching, a sensible code of practice needs to be adhered to so that there is no disturbance. Such a code exists (*www.wisescheme.org*) but keeping to it is what really matters.

Much the same can be said for seals. They spend a large amount of the day basking on rocks or on the shore at Rathlin. In Mill Bay and at Rue Point they are easily observed and approaches by land and sea can also spook them. Watch seals for a while and you see them dry out and change colour from dark grey of wet fur to pale grey with spots, fawn, buff, brown. You would not be too happy if you were chased from your beach deck chair as you lie in warm sun, also changing colour. Common sense dictates keep a good distance, bring a pair of binoculars and have a lens on your camera that enables photos to be taken from medium range. The bird buses drop off viewers to see the Mill Bay seals and here is an opportunity for a bit of guidance on sensible behaviour by those passengers wanting to see the seals.

Walking Routes

Several routes have been developed on Rathlin and these are well promoted. There is walking information in the island's ferry terminal or on the island you can enquire at the boathouse information centre or in the souvenir shop, while accommodation providers on the island also have information about these walks. The three lighthouse walks are all on roads; to the west light, to the east light and to the south light. Access to the lighthouses is not possible at present (2010) without special permission from the Commissioners of Irish Lights (HQ in Dublin) but this is not necessary to enjoy the views and the wildlife. Provided walkers keep to these roads, then this is a robust and sustainable way to see parts of the island.

Off-road walks on Rathlin are limited at present to two areas. The NT owns Ballyconagan townland, off the route to the east light, and has a circular excursion here, with magnificent views, fascinating flora and an abandoned settlement or *clachan*. It does, however, pass through sensitive habitats such as wetlands and dry heath, so it may not be sustainable if there were large numbers of users over the flowering season and walkers were to wander at will. The RSPB has developed a circular walk on the south arm of the island at Roonivoolin, with a variety of coastal scenery and wildlife. Good way-marking, well maintained, is essential if users are not to cause disturbance to wildlife and stock. There are a few other cliff-top viewpoints with permitted access. Most of the rest of Rathlin is private land, much of it farmed. There are also valuable nature sites and historic monuments . Many of these are on private land while some have access allowed, but at present it is not always clear where you can walk at these designated areas. It is best to enquire locally.

What should I do, or not do?

Refer to the *Rathlin Code* which is available on the island and is published in the leaflet *Rathlin Island: A Hidden Treasure*.

Common sense goes a long way. Don't try to get too close to wild animals, birds or farm stock. Do by all means take photos, but don't 'garden' around a flower or any plant to improve your picture. Don't try to make the living subject (animal, bird, insect or whatever) do something to enhance your photos. Do take the guidebook to the plants or animals. Don't pick the plants or collect the animals (the little ones) – the big ones can take care of themselves pretty well.

Trampling, even a little, damages vegetation so keep to obvious paths. Close gates after you. Don't climb walls, many on Rathlin are dry stone walls and are easily broken apart. Respect 'Private' and similar signs. If a sign says 'bull', it usually means it, but it also may mean 'we'd rather you kept out.'

If you do take a boat trip or any form of guided tour and you feel that there is disturbance being caused or something isn't right, speak out. You can experience a lot of freedom on Rathlin. Do not abuse this – it's a rare privilege, most of it granted by landowners and conservation bodies. Rathlin islanders care a lot about their home place. Some are more open about their views than others, and it is important to respect their feelings. Be diplomatic; respect has to be earned here and if you get it right you can be sure of a warm welcome any time.

REFERENCES

Anson, P.F. 1965. *Fisher Folk-Lore.* The Faith Press, London.

Armstrong, E.A. 1940. *Birds of the Grey Wind.* Oxford University Press, London.

Baldwin, J. In press. *Harvesting Seabirds and their Eggs on the Irish Sea Islands (Part 4).* Folk Life: Journal of Ethnological Studies, Vol. 49, No.2.

Ballard, L-M. 1983. *Seal Stories and Belief on Rathlin Island.* Ulster Folklife, Volume 29, pp. 33-42.

Ballard, L-M. 1997. *Fairies and the Supernatural on Reachrai.* In, *The Good People – New Fairylore and Essays.* Ed. Peter Narváez, The University Press, Kentucky.

Ballard, L-M. 2000-2001. *Thomas Cecil, the Compleat Islandman?* Folklife, Volume 39, 2000-2001, pp. 32-48.

Barne, J.H. *et.al.* (eds.) 1997. *Coasts and seas of the United Kingdom, Region 17. Northern Ireland.* Joint Nature Conservation Committee, Peterborough.

Berry, R.J. 1977. *Inheritance and Natural History.* New Naturalist (Number 61). Collins, London.

Berry, R.J. 2009. *Islands.* New Naturalist (Number 109). HarperCollins, London.

Boyd, H.A. 1947. *Rathlin Island, North of Antrim.* J.S.Scarlett and Son, Ballycastle, County Antrim.

Breen J., Hanna J., and Harrison T. 2006. *A Survey of the Marine Environment of Rathlin Island.* Report, 81 pp. Conservation Science, Environment and Heritage Service, Department of the Environment for Northern Ireland, Belfast.

Briggs, K. 1979. *Abbey Lubbers, Banshees and Boggarts – A Who's Who of Fairies.* Kestrel Books, Middlesex.

Cabot, D. 1999. *Ireland: A Natural History.* New Naturalist (Number 84), HarperCollins, London.

Campbell, M. 1951. *Sea Wrack, or Long-ago Tales of Rathlin Island.* J.S.Scarlett and Son, Ballycastle, County Antrim.

Cecil, T. 1990. *The Harsh Winds of Rathlin: Stories of Rathlin's Shipwrecks.* Impact Printing, Coleraine, County Londonderry.

Clark, W. 1996. (6th edition). *Rathlin –Its Island Story*. Impact Printing, Coleraine, County Londonderry.

Corson, T. 2005. *The Secret Life of Lobsters*. Harper Perennial, New York.

Curran, B. 1997. *A Field Guide to Irish Fairies*. Appletree Press, Belfast.

Davey, B. 2006. *Rathlin, An Island Odyssey*. Cottage Publications, Donaghadee, County Down.

Day, A., McWilliams, P. And Dobson, N. (Eds.). 1994. *Ordnance Survey Memoirs of Ireland, Volume 24, Parishes of County Antrim IX, 1830-2, 1835, 1838-9. North Antrim Coast and Rathlin*. The Institute of Irish Studies, The Queen's University of Belfast.

Deegan, G. 2010. *On the front line to save the corncrake*. The Irish Times, September 11, 2010, Weekend Review, p.6.

Dickson, J.M. 2008. *A Flora of Rathlin Island*. Impact Printing, Coleraine, County Londonderry.

Easpaig, D.M. 1989-90. *The Place-Names of Rathlin Island*. AINM Bulletin of the Ulster Place-Name Society, Volume IV, pp. 3-89. Belfast.

Elwood, J.H. 1971. *A Demographic Study of Tory Island and Rathlin Island*. Ulster Folklife, Volume 17, pp.70-80.

Erwin, D. G., Picton, B.E. *Et.al.* 1990. *Inshore Marine Life of Northern Ireland*. Department of the Environment for Northern Ireland. HMSO, Belfast.

Evans, E.E. 1957. *Irish Folk Ways*. Routledge and Kegan Paul. (6th impression, 1976, Routledge Paperback).

Evans, G.E. and Thomson, D. 2002. *The Leaping Hare*. Faber and Faber, London.

Ewing, J.H. 1896. *The Brownies and Other Tales*. George Bell and Sons, London.

Fairley, J.S. 1975. *An Irish Beast Book: A natural history of Ireland's furred wildlife*. Blackstaff Press Limited, Belfast.

Fenton, A. 2008. *The Sea-Vocabulary of Fishermen in the Northern Isles*, in *Scottish Life and Society, A Compendium of Scottish Ethnology*, Volume 4, *Boats, Fishing* *and the Sea.* Eds. James R Coull, Alexander Fenton and Kenneth Veitch. John Donald, Edinburgh.

Forsythe, W. 2006. *The Archaeology of the Kelp Industry in the Northern Islands of Ireland.* The International Journal of Nautical Archaeology, Volume 35, pp. 218-229.

Forsythe, W. 2007. *On the Edge of Improvement: Rathlin Island and the Modern World.* Journal of Historical Archaeology, Volume 11, pp. 221-240.

Franzen, J. 2010. *Emptying the Skies. A Reporter at Large.* The New Yorker, July 26, 2010, pp. 48-61.

Gage, C. 1851. *A History of the Island of Rathlin.* Manuscript (hand-written). Published in 1995 by Dickson, J. M., Impact Printing, Coleraine, County Londonderry.

Gill, A. 1993. *Superstitions: Folk Magic in Hull's Fishing Community.* Hutton Press Limited, North Humberside.

Goodwin, C., Edwards, H., Breen J. and Picton, B. 2010. *Rathlin Island: A Survey Report from the Nationally Important Marine Features Project 2009-2011.* 38 pp. Northern Ireland Environment Agency, Department of the Environment for Northern Ireland, Belfast, and National Museums Northern Ireland.

Greer, J. 1994. *Living on an Island: An Integrated Study of Rathlin.* Drumnamallaght Press, Ballymoney, County Antrim.

Habitas (on-line). www.habitas.org/literature (search key word = Rathlin Island)

Hackney, P. (Ed.), 1992. *Stewart and Corry's Flora of the North-East of Ireland.* The Institute of Irish Studies, Queen's University of Belfast.

Hamilton, W. 1790. *Letters Concerning The Northern Coast Of The County Of Antrim...*Dublin and London.

Hayes, R.J. (Ed.). *Articles in Irish Periodicals.* Volume 9, pp. (Rathlin, pp 86 *et.seq.*). G.K.Hall and Company, Boston, Mass.

Joyce, P.W. 1910. *The Origin And History Of Irish Names Of Places*. Three volumes, Longmans, Green, and Company, London, and M.H.Gill and Son, Dublin.

Kingsley, C. 1855. *Westward Ho!* Andrew Melrose, London.

Law, H.I. 1961. *Rathlin, Island and Parish*. The Mid-Ulster Printing Company Limited, Cookstown, County Tyrone.

Lyle, P. 2010. *Between Rocks and Hard Places: Discovering Ireland's Northern Landscapes*. Geological Survey of Northern Ireland, Belfast.

Mabey, R. 1996. *Flora Brittanica*. Sinclair-Stevenson, London.

Mabey, R. 2010. *Weeds*. Profile Books, London.

MacCoitir, N. 2006. *Irish Wild Plants: Myths, Legends and Folklore*. The Collins Press, Cork.

MacCoitir, N. 2010. *Ireland's Animals: Myths, Legends and Folklore*. The Collins Press, Cork.

MacNeice, L. 1938. *I Crossed The Minch*. Longmans, Green and Company (Re-issued by Polygon, Edinburg, 2007).

Marshall, J.D. 1836. *Notes on the statistics and natural history of the Island of Rathlin, off the northern coast of Ireland*. Royal Irish Academy Transactions, Volume XVII, Antiquities, pp. 37-71 (1832-37).

Martin, A. 1984. *Kintyre: The Hidden Past*. John Donald Publications Limited, Edinburgh.

McCurdy, A. 2010. *An Island Childhood; Growing Up on Rathlin Island*, Published by the author, Rathlin Island, Co. Antrim.

McCurdy, A. 2006. *Stories and Legends of Rathlin*. Impact Printing, Coleraine, County Londonderry.

McCurdy, A. 2007. *Gaeílge Reachlann:A History of Rathlin Irish*. Published by the author, Rathlin Island, County Antrim.

McCurdy, A. (Undated) *Walking on Rathlin Island*. Published by the author, Rathlin Island, County Antrim.

McCurdy, A. 2000. *Rathlin's Rugged Story from an islander's perspective.* Impact Printing, Coleraine, County Londonderry.

Morrison, M. 2003. *Rathlin As I Knew It.* Published by the author, Ballycastle, County Antrim.

Murphy, M.J. 1987. *Rathlin: Island of Blood and Enchantment, The Folklore of Rathlin.* Dundalgan Press (W.Tempest) Limited, Dundalk, County Louth.

Nelson, B. And Thompson, R. 2004. *The Natural History of Ireland's Dragonflies.* The National Museums and Galleries of Northern Ireland, Belfast.

Newton, I. 2010. *Bird Migration.* New Naturalist (number 113), Collins, London.

Ó hÓgáin, D. 2006. *The Lore of Ireland. An Encyclopaedia of Myth, Legend and Romance.* The Collins Press, Cork.

O'Sullivan, M. and Downey, L. 2010. *Seaweeds and Kelp.* Archaeology Ireland, Volume 24, Number 3, Issue 93, pp. 37-40.

Quagliana, P. 1999. *Shoot on a treasure island.* Shooting Times and Country Magazine, 11 March 1999, pp.40-43.

Rathlin Island Development and Community Association, 2011. *Rathlin Island: A Hidden Treasure.* www.rathlincommunity.org

Seasearch, 2005, 2007. www.seasearch.org.uk

Stevenson, R. 1982. *Some Memories of Life on Rathlin Sixty Years Ago.* The Glynns, Journal of the Glens of Antrim Historical Association, Volume 10, pp. 40-46.

Stone, C.J., Webb, A. Et.al. 1995. *An atlas of seabird distribution in north-west European waters.* Joint Nature Conservation Committee, Peterborough.

Taylor, R.M. 2004. *The Lighthouse of Ireland: A Personal History.* The Collins Press, Cork.

The Islands Book Trust, 2005. *Traditions of Sea-Bird Fowling in the North Atlantic Region.* The Islands Book Trust, Port of Ness, Isle of Lewis, Scotland.

Thompson, R and Nelson, B. 2006. *The Butterflies and Moths of Northern Ireland.* National Museums Northern Ireland, Belfast.

Thomson, D. 1965. *The People of the Sea: A Journey in Search of the Seal Legend.* Barrie and Rockliff, London.

Tourism Development International and Judith Annett Countryside Consultancy, 2005. *Rathlin Island Sustainable Tourism Strategy 2005-2015.* Report.

Vickery, R. 2010. *Garlands, Conkers and Mother-Die: British and Irish Plant Lore.* Continuum UK, London.

Watson, G. 2007. *Monitoring Seabirds on Rathlin Island.* EHS Coast, Issue Number 2, 2007,pp. 13-14. Environment and Heritage Service, Department of the Environment for Northern Ireland, Belfast.

Watson, P.S. 2004. *A Companion to the Causeway Coast Way.* The Blackstaff Press Limited, Belfast, for Environment and Heritage Service, Department of the Environment for Northern Ireland.

Watson, P.S. 2009. *Strange Behaviours: A History of Naturalists and Nature Studies in the Glens of Antrim.* The Glynns, Journal of the Glens of Antrim Historical Society, Volume 37, pp. 32-54.

Watson, P.S. 1980. *The Seabirds of Northern Ireland and Adjacent Waters.* Irish Birds, Volume 1, pp. 462-486.

Wilson, H.E. and Robbie, J.A. 1966. *Geology of the Country Around Ballycastle.* Memoir Number 8, Geological Survey of Northern Ireland, HMSO, Belfast.

ACKNOWLEDGEMENTS

Over the 50 years I've been visiting Rathlin, many people there have supplied information, provided hospitality and friendship or just helped in various ways. Some islanders and former residents I left in peace and asked no questions and others have written books and booklets about their island home which I found most helpful – notably Tommy Cecil, Catherine Gage, Augustus McCurdy and Alex Morrison, and also Mary Campbell, who had close Rathlin connections. I hope that I might be forgiven if anyone feels left out.

Those mentioned below marked with an asterisk* are, sadly, deceased. On the island, I thank the McFauls: Mary* senior, Danny* Peggy, Neil, Jim, Liam, Alison, John, Benjy, Emma and Mary. Also, thanks to the Cecils: Dougal*, Bridget*, Vincent*, Tommy*, Mary, Douglas and Rosaleen. Thanks as well to the following McCurdys: John and Jennifer, Noel and Peter. Other islanders whom I thank are Babs O'Connor, Richard and Angela Green, Bertie and Johnny Curry, and various staff at the Manor House over the years. Frances and Ezekiel Gage provided hospitality and access to some rare books and manuscripts, all much appreciated. I'm grateful to wildlife photographer Tom McDonnell for help in many ways, and also to David Quinney Mee, Catriona Blaney and Jessica Bates.

On the mainland, my thanks to Linda-May Ballard, Curator of Folk Life of the Ulster Folk and Transport Museum, for her help and encouragement, and Roger Dixon, Librarian at UFTM for sourcing various references. Members of the staff at the Linenhall Library in Belfast were helpful in finding information for me. Thanks to Joe Breen of the Northern Ireland Environment Agency for supplying reports and information on diving and other marine surveys, and to Clare Dore of the Department of Agriculture and Rural Development who provided details of farming on the island and a list of current agri-environment schemes. At the Geological Survey of Northern Ireland, thanks are due to Garth Earls (now with Dalradian Gold) and Paul Lyle. I thank Wes Forsythe and Tom McErlean of the Maritime Archaeology Unit at the University of Ulster (Coleraine) for information at various times. Other individuals thanked are: Dave Allen, John Baldwin, Hugh A Boyd*, Cahal Dallat*, Professor JS Fairley and John E Greer.* A special thanks to Tom Ennis, who first invited me to Rathlin to help set up the Bird Observatory and for early guidance in the skills of bird identification.

The Commissioners of Irish Lights, and a number of their lighthouse-keepers, are thanked for accommodation and assistance many years ago. I am grateful to Rathlin Island Ferries Limited for getting me on and off the island, sometimes in difficult conditions. Prior to their existence, I relied on island boatmen and, on the mainland, Jack Coyles*, all of whom are thanked.

A number of organisations have employed me or otherwise supported my work on Rathlin and I mention these for both this privilege and for other assistance: the Fisheries Research Laboratory of the former Ministry of Agriculture, the Royal Society for the Protection of Birds, Northern Ireland 2000, Enterprise Ulster, the Rathlin Island Trust, the National Trust, Moyle District Council, Northern Ireland Environment Agency and Allen and Mellon Environmental.

This book has been a family project: my son and publisher John Stewart Watson, founder and the force behind *Stone Country*, has been a constant source of encouragement and support and first came to Rathlin with me aged 5 and saw the bottle-nosed whale; my daughter Kari, creator and managing director of *O-Communications* has been a great help with proof-reading and publicity, and my wife Kay has put up with my absences and my island obsession for a long time. I thank all of them very much.

PHOTOGRAPHIC ACKNOWLEDGMENTS

We are grateful to Tom McDonnell for his wildlife and landscape photographs; to Esler Crawford for the aerial photograph on the cover, which appeared on his own book *The North: A View From the Skies* published by Blackstaff Press in 2008; to Loughie McQuaig for the photograph of horse ploughing on Rathlin from the Boathouse Museum and to John McCurdy (and the Boathouse Committee) and Tom McDonnell for help with sourcing this; to Tommy McDonald for the bird hunters photograph; to Alan Watson for the dragonfly picture; to Joe Breen of Northern Ireland Environment Agency for the underwater photographs. In the latter, the sonar image of Rathlin's north sub-marine coast is from the Joint Irish Bathymetric Survey (JIBS), supported by the Interreg programme. The remainder of the photographs were taken by the author.

APPENDIX 1

Seabird Counts on Rathlin Island, 1999 > 2007

- **FULMAR**   2032 >1072
  Counts are in units of Apparently Occupied Sites

- **GULLS**   591 > 185
  Totals of 5 species: Herring, Greater Black-backed, Lesser Black-backed, Common and Black Headed. All counts in units of Apparently Occupied Nests.

- **KITTIWAKE**   9917 > 9896
  Counts are in units of Apparently Occupied Nests

- **GUILLEMOT**   95567 > 81303
  Counts are in units of Individuals

- **RAZORBILL**   20860 > 10684
  Counts are in units of Individuals

- **PUFFIN**   1579 > 731
  Counts are in units of Individuals

- **BLACK GUILLEMOT**   227 > 101*
  Counts are in units of Individuals. (*2001 was the closest comparative count to 2007).

- **SHAG**   58 > 46
  Counts are in units of Apparently Occupied Nests

APPENDIX 2

Conservation Designations

Designation of sites may happen at an international, national and regional/local level. At Rathlin Island, the following conservation designations apply:

- **Special Protection Area (SPA)** The whole island and an area of the sea, totalling 3345 hectares.
- **Special Area of Conservation (SAC)** Same area and boundaries as for SPA, totalling 3345 hectares.
- **National Nature Reserve (NNR)** Kebble and cliffs in the west of the island.
- **Areas of Special Scientific Interest (ASSI)** Rathlin's coast and three other land areas, totalling about 400 hectares.
- **Area of Outstanding Natural Beauty (AONB)** Rathlin is included in the Antrim Coast and Glens AONB.

Further designations, including those relevant to the built heritage, and other useful information can be found at:

- **Northern Ireland Environment Agency (NIEA)** www.ni-environment.gov.uk
- **The National Trust** www.nationaltrust.org.uk
- **Causeway Coast and Glens Heritage Trust** www.ccght.org
- **Royal Society for the Protection of Birds** www.rspb.org
- **National Museums of Northern Ireland** www.nmni.com
- **Coleraine University Centre for Maritime Archaeology**
  www.science.ac.uk/esri/Centre-for-Maritime-Archaeology
- **www.wisescheme.org**

GLOSSARY OF SOME LOCAL WORDS

- **Bo/Bow** - An underwater reef, a word of Norse origin.
- **Clachan** - A small settlement; a cluster of homes - which can be part of a farming community.
- **Cudden** -The younger stages of the Coalfish or Glashan.
- **Doll** or **Dull** - Snares used to trap seabirds ashore on rocky areas and cliffs.
- **Donal Gorm** - A Rathlin name for the sea.
- **Frassing/Frass Holes** -To throw out a mix of bait to attract fish when fishing by line, usually from the shore. A frass hole is a hollow in the rocks were this bait is ground into small pieces.
- **Ghostyn** - Another word for above snares.
- **Glashan** - The coalfish, a member of the cod family.
- **Lythe** - The Pollack, a member of the cod family.
- **Meith** - An alignment of landmarks that helps fishermen locate known fishing areas.
- **Moran** or **Mearn** - Pronounced and generally used as 'murran'. The Ballan Wrasse, a fish found both inshore and in deeper water around Rathlin's marine waters.
- **Parrots** - Formerly used by Rathlin's cliff climbers to describe the auks, namely puffin, razorbill and guillemot, hunted for food or for their eggs prior to 1945.
- **Raghery** - An old name for Rathlin, still occasionally used locally.
- **Sea of Moyle** - The waters around Rathlin – the general boundaries being Malin Head in the west, Islay in Scotland to the north, Lough Ryan in Scotland to the east and south to Larne in County Antrim.
- **Stuey** - A commercial fishing line float, formerly made of inflated cured dog skin, then canvas. Most floats now are of strong plastic construction and the name is no longer in use.